TEACHER'S GUIDE

daybook, *n*. a book in
which the events of
the day are
recorded; *specif.* a
journal or diary

DAYBOOK

of Critical Reading and Writing

GRADE 7

CONSULTING AUTHORS

FRAN CLAGGETT

LOUANN REID

RUTH VINZ

Great Source Education Group
a Houghton Mifflin Company
Wilmington, Massachusetts

www.greatsource.com

Consulting Authors

Fran Claggett, currently an educational consultant for schools throughout the country and teacher at Sonoma State University, taught high school English for more than thirty years. She is author of several books, including *Drawing Your Own Conclusions: Graphic Strategies for Reading, Writing, and Thinking* (1992) and *A Measure of Success* (1996).

Louann Reid taught junior and senior high school English, speech, and drama for nineteen years and currently teaches courses for future English teachers at Colorado State University. Author of numerous articles and chapters, her first books were *Learning the Landscape* and *Recasting the Text* with Fran Claggett and Ruth Vinz (1996).

Ruth Vinz, currently a professor and director of English education at Teachers College, Columbia University, taught in secondary schools for twenty-three years. She is author of several books and numerous articles that discuss teaching and learning in the English classroom as well as a frequent presenter, consultant, and co-teacher in schools throughout the country.

Printed in the United States of America

International Standard Book Number: 0-669-46788-X

7 8 9 10 -POO- 04 03 02

Great Source wishes to acknowledge the many insights and improvements made to the *Daybooks* thanks to the work of the following teachers and educators.

R e a d e r s

Jay Amberg
Glenbrook South High School
Glenview, Illinois

Joanne Arellanes
Rancho Cordova, California

Nancy Bass
Moore Middle School
Arvada, Colorado

Jim Benny
Sierra Mountain Middle School
Truckee, California

Noreen Benton
Guilderland High School
Altamont, New York

Janet Bertucci
Hawthorne Junior High School
Vernon Hills, Illinois

Jim Burke
Burlingame High School
Burlingame, California

Mary Castellano
Hawthorne Junior High School
Vernon Hills, Illinois

Diego Davalos
Chula Vista High School
Chula Vista, California

Jane Detgen
Daniel Wright Middle School
Lake Forest, Illinois

Michelle Ditzian
Shepard Junior High School
Deerfield, Illinois

Jenni Dunlap
Highland Middle School
Libertyville, Illinois

Judy Elman
Highland Park High School
Highland Park, Illinois

Mary Ann Evans-Patrick
Fox Valley Writing Project
Oshkosh, Wisconsin

Howard Frishman
Twin Grove Junior High School
Buffalo Grove, Illinois

Kathleen Gaynor
Wheaton, Illinois

Beatrice Gerrish
Bell Middle School
Golden, Colorado

Kathy Glass
San Carlos, California

Alton Greenfield
Minnesota Dept. of Child,
Family & Learning
St. Paul, Minnesota

Sue Hebson
Deerfield High School
Deerfield, Illinois

Carol Jago
Santa Monica High School
Santa Monica, California

Diane Kepner
Oakland, California

Lynne Ludwig
Gregory Middle School
Naperville, Illinois

Joan Markos-Horejs
Fox Valley Writing Project
Oshkosh, Wisconsin

James McDermott
South High Community School
Worcester, Massachusetts

Tim McGee
Worland High School
Worland, Wyoming

Mary Jane Mulholland
Lynn Classical High School
Lynn, Massachusetts

Lisa Myers
Englewood, Colorado

Karen Neilsen
Desert Foothills Middle School
Phoenix, Arizona

Jayne Allen Nichols
El Camino High School
Sacramento, California

Mary Nicolini
Penn Harris High School
Mishawaka, Indiana

Lucretia Pannozzo
John Jay Middle School
Katonah, New York

Robert Pavlick
Marquette University
Milwaukee, Wisconsin

Linda Popp
Gregory Middle School
Naperville, Illinois

Caroline Ratliffe
Fort Bend Instructional School District
Sugar Land, Texas

Guerrino Rich
Akron North High School
Akron, Ohio

Shirley Rosson
Alief Instructional School District
Houston, Texas

Alan Ruter
Glenbrook South High School
Glenview, Illinois

Rene Schillenger
Washington, D.C.

Georgianne Schulte
Oak Park Middle School
Oak Park, Illinois

Carol Schultz
Tinley Park, Illinois

Wendell Schwartz
Adlai E. Stevenson High School
Lincolnshire, Illinois

Lynn Snell
Oak Grove School
Green Oaks, Illinois

Hildi Spritzer
Oakland, California

Bill Stone
Plano Senior High School
Plano, Texas

Barbara Thompson
Hazelwood School
Florissant, Missouri

Elma Torres
Orange Grove Instructional
School District
Orange Grove, Texas

Bill Weber
Libertyville High School
Libertyville, Illinois

Darby Williams
Sacramento, California

Hillary Zunin
Napa High School
Napa, California

Table of Contents

Overview

What is a daybook and what is it good for? These are the first questions asked about this series, *Daybooks of Critical Reading and Writing*.

The answer is that a daybook is a keepable, journal-like book that helps improve students' reading and writing. *Daybooks* are a tool to promote daily reading and writing in classrooms. By immersing students in good literature and by asking them to respond creatively to it, the *Daybooks* combine critical reading and creative, personal response to literature.

The literature in each *Daybook* has been chosen to complement the selections commonly found in anthologies and the most commonly taught novels. Most of the literature selections are brief and designed to draw students into them by their brevity and high-interest appeal. In addition, each passage has a literary quality that will be probed in the lesson.

Each lesson focuses on a specific aspect of critical reading—that is, the reading skills used by good readers. These aspects of critical reading are summarized in closing statements positioned at the end of each lesson. To organize this wide-ranging analysis into critical reading, the consulting authors have constructed a framework called the "Angles of Literacy."

This framework organizes the lessons and units in the *Daybook*. The five Angles of Literacy described here are:

- marking or annotating the text
- examining the story connections
- looking at authors' perspectives
- studying the language and craft of a text
- focusing on individual authors

The Angles of Literacy are introduced in the first cluster of the *Daybook* and then explored in greater depth in subsequent clusters.

The *Daybook* concept was developed to help teachers with a number of practical concerns:

1. To introduce daily (or at least weekly) critical reading and writing into classrooms

2. To fit into the new configurations offered by block scheduling

3. To create a literature book students can own, allowing them to mark up the literature and write as they read

4. To make an affordable literature book that students can carry home

How to Use the Daybook

As the *Daybooks* were being developed, more than fifty teachers commented on and reviewed the lesson concept and individual lessons and units. Middle school teachers helped shape the choice of literature and the skills to be taught. From their efforts and our discussions, several main uses for the *Daybooks* emerged.

1. Supplementing an Anthology

For literature teachers stuck with dated anthologies, the *Daybooks* appeared to offer an easy, economical means of updating their literature curriculums. The multitude of contemporary authors and wide range of multicultural authors fit nicely with older and soon-to-become out-of-date anthology series.

2. Supplementing a List of Core Novels

For middle schools guided by a list of core readings, the *Daybooks* offered a convenient way to add some daily writing and critical reading instruction to classes. Plus, the emphasis on newer, young adult writers seemed to these teachers just right for their courses laden with "classics."

3. Adding a New Element

Some middle school teachers use the *Daybooks* to add literature to their curriculum; some use them to add an element of critical reading to what is already a literature-based approach; other teachers rely on the *Daybooks* to add the element of daily reading and writing to their curriculum. Teachers have found a number of different ways to slot the *Daybooks* into their curriculums, mostly because of their three-way combination of literature, critical reading, and daily creative writing.

4. Block Scheduling

Daybook activities were also designed to accommodate new block-scheduled class periods. With longer periods, teachers commented on the need to introduce 2-4 parts to each "block," one of which would be a *Daybook* lesson. The brief, self-contained lessons fit perfectly at the beginning or end of a block and could be used to complement or build upon another segment of the day.

The reviewers of the *Daybooks* proved that no two classrooms are alike. While each was unique in its own way, every teacher found use for the *Daybook* lessons in the classroom. In the end, the usefulness of the *Daybooks* derived from the blend of elements they alone offer:

- direct instruction of how to read critically
- regular and explicit practice in marking up and annotating texts
- "writing to learn" activities for each day or week
- great selections from contemporary (and often multicultural) literature
- in-depth instruction in how to read literature and write effectively about it

Organization of the Daybooks

Each *Daybook* has 14 units, or clusters, of five lessons. A lesson is designed to last approximately 30 minutes, although some lessons will surely extend longer depending on how energetically students attack the writing activities. But the intent throughout was to create brief, potent lessons that integrate quality literature, critical reading instruction, and writing.

The unifying concept behind these lessons is the Angles of Literacy—the idea that a selection can be approached from at least five directions:

- by annotating and marking up the text
- by analyzing the story connections in the literature
- by examining authors' perspectives
- by studying the language and craft of the writer
- by focusing closely on all of the aspects of a single writer's work

A lesson typically begins with an introduction and leads quickly into a literary selection. By looking closely at the selection, students are able to discover what can be learned through careful reading. Students are led to look again at the selection and to respond analytically, reflectively, and creatively to what they have read. An Answer Key at the back of this book provides selected sample responses.

boldface terms in glossary

onomatopoeia, words that sound like what they mean. Examples: buzz, crackle, hiss.

inion, a person's personal ideas ab...

focus on critical reading

lesson title

unit title

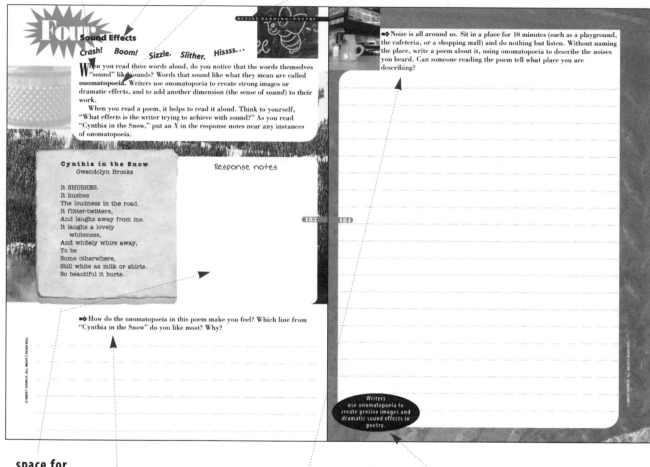

ACTIVE READING: POETRY

Focus

Sound Effects

Crash! Boom! Sizzle. Slither. Hissss...

When you read these words aloud, do you notice that the words themselves "sound" like sounds? Words that sound like what they mean are called **onomatopoeia.** Writers use onomatopoeia to create strong images or dramatic effects, and to add another dimension (the sense of *sound*) to their work.

When you read a poem, it helps to read it aloud. Think to yourself, "What effects is the writer trying to achieve with sound?" As you read "Cynthia in the Snow," put an X in the response notes near any instances of onomatopoeia.

Cynthia in the Snow
Gwendolyn Brooks

It SHUSHES.
It hushes
The loudness in the road.
It flitter-twitters,
And laughs away from me.
It laughs a lovely
    whiteness,
And whitely whirs away,
To be
Some otherwhere,
Still white as milk or shirts.
So beautiful it hurts.

Response notes

➔ How do the onomatopoeia in this poem make you feel? Which line from "Cynthia in the Snow" do you like most? Why?

➔ Noise is all around us. Sit in a place for 10 minutes (such as a playground, the cafeteria, or a shopping mall) and do nothing but listen. Without naming the place, write a poem about it, using onomatopoeia to describe the noises you heard. Can someone reading the poem tell what place you are describing?

Writers use onomatopoeia to create precise images and dramatic sound effects in poetry.

space for annotations

longer, interpretive response to literature

summary statement

initial response activity

F r e q u e n t l y   A s k e d   Q u e s t i o n s

One benefit of the extensive field-testing of the *Daybooks* was to highlight right at the beginning several questions about the *Daybooks*.

1. What is a daybook anyway?

A daybook used to be "a book in which daily transactions are recorded" or "a diary." Most recently, the word has been used to mean "journal." To emphasize the daily reading and writing, the authors chose the word *daybook* rather than *journal*. And, indeed, the *Daybooks* are much more than journals, in that they include literature selections and instruction in critical reading.

2. Are students supposed to write in the *Daybook*?

Yes, definitely. Only by physically marking the text will students become active readers. To interact with a text and take notes as an active reader, students must write in their *Daybooks*. Students will have a written record of their thoughts, questions, brainstorms, annotations, and creative responses. The immediacy of reading and responding on the page is an integral feature of the *Daybooks*. Students will also benefit from the notebook-like aspect, allowing them to double back to earlier work, see progress, store ideas, and record responses. The *Daybook* serves, in a way, like a portfolio. It is one simple form of portfolio assessment.

3. Can I photocopy these lessons?

No, unfortunately, you cannot. The selections, instruction, and activities are protected by copyright. To copy them infringes on the rights of the authors of the selections and the book. Writers such as Langston Hughes, Cynthia Rylant, and Ray Bradbury have granted permission for the use of their work in the *Daybooks* and to photocopy their work violates their copyright.

4. Can I skip around in the *Daybook*?

Yes, absolutely. The *Daybooks* were designed to allow teachers maximum flexibility. You can start with some of the later clusters (or units) and then pick up the earlier ones later on in the year. Or you can teach a lesson from here and one from there. But the optimum order of the book is laid out in the table of contents, and students will most likely see the logic and continuity of the book when they start at the beginning and proceed in order.

5. What is "annotating a text"? Are students supposed to write in the margin of the book?

Annotating refers to underlining parts of a text, circling words or phrases, highlighting with a colored marker, or taking notes in the margin. Students begin their school years marking up books in kindergarten and end, often in college, writing in the margins of their texts or highlighting key passages. Yet in the years in between—the majority of their school years—students are often forbidden from writing in their books, even though it represents a natural kinesthetic aid for memory and learning.

6. Why were these literature selections chosen?

The literature was chosen primarily for its high interest for students. Middle school teachers advised the editors how to construct a table of contents that had the selections with proven student appeal. The first, and foremost, criterion was the appeal of a selection for students.

But the literature was also carefully matched with the lesson concept. (A lesson on characters, for example, needed to present two or three strong characters for study.) So, in addition to high student appeal, the selections illustrate a specific aspect of critical reading and are representative of the diversity of our society.

7. What are the art and photos supposed to represent?

The art program for the *Daybooks* features the work of outstanding contemporary photographers. These photos open each unit and set the tone. Then, within each lesson, a number of smaller, somewhat enigmatic images are used. The purpose behind these images is not to illustrate what is happening in the literature or even to represent an interpretation of it. Rather, the hope is to stretch students' minds, hinting at connections, provoking the imagination, jarring loose a random thought or two about the selection. And, of course, the hope is that students will respond favorably to contemporary expressions of creativity.

8. In what way do the *Daybooks* teach critical thinking skills?

One of the hallmarks of the middle school *Daybooks* is their emphasis on critical reading skills, such as predicting, inferencing, and evaluating. On the advice of practicing teachers, the middle school *Daybooks* purposely emphasized the key skills students need to improve their reading skills, such as finding the main idea, distinguishing fact from opinion, making inferences, reflecting on what you read, and so forth. In fact, critical thinking skills are taught across the grades, as the scope and sequence chart in this guide on pages 11-12 shows. The *Daybooks* are a marriage of strong teaching of critical reading skills with good literature and the consistent opportunity to write about what you read.

9. What are the boldface terms in the lesson all about?

The terms boldfaced in the lessons appear in the back of the *Daybook*. The glossary includes key literary terms that 1) are used in the *Daybook* lessons, and 2) students are likely to encounter in literature classes. The glossary is another resource for students to use in reading and reacting to the literature.

Skill Instruction	Grade 6	Grade 7	Grade 8
Comprehension			
author's perspective/viewpoint	✓	✓	✓
author's purpose	✓	✓	✓
bias	✓	✓	
cause and effect	✓	✓	✓
change pace	✓		✓
compare and contrast	✓	✓	✓
details	✓	✓	✓
draw conclusions		✓	✓
evaluate	✓	✓	✓
fact and opinion	✓	✓	✓
generalize		✓	✓
inference	✓	✓	✓
make connections to personal life	✓	✓	✓
predict	✓	✓	✓
reflect	✓	✓	✓
respond to literature	✓	✓	✓
sequence	✓		
summarize	✓		✓
thesis statement	✓	✓	✓
visualize		✓	✓
Literary Elements/Author's Craft			
alliteration	✓		✓
author's style	✓	✓	✓
characterization	✓	✓	✓
imagery	✓	✓	
irony	✓	✓	✓
metaphor	✓	✓	✓
mood	✓	✓	
onomatopoeia		✓	
personification	✓	✓	✓
plot	✓	✓	✓
point of view	✓	✓	✓
repetition, rhyme, rhythm	✓	✓	✓
sensory language	✓	✓	✓
setting	✓	✓	✓
simile	✓	✓	✓
symbolism		✓	
text structure	✓	✓	✓
theme	✓	✓	✓
tone	✓	✓	✓
word choice	✓	✓	✓

Skill Instruction	Grade 6	Grade 7	Grade 8
Study and Word Skills			
formulate questions	✓	✓	
highlight	✓	✓	✓
preview	✓		✓
take notes	✓	✓	✓
use context clues	✓		
use graphic sources	✓	✓	✓
use structural clues	✓	✓	✓

Correlation to Write Source 2000

Like the *Write Source 2000* handbook, the *Daybooks* will appeal to certain teachers who need versatile, flexible materials and who place a premium on books with high student appeal. Some teachers, by nature, are more eclectic in their teaching approach, and others are more consistent and patterned. Some teachers place a premium on student interest and relevance more than on structured, predictable lessons. The *Daybooks*, like *Write Source 2000*, are directed at more eclectic teachers and classrooms.

The *Daybooks* are organized to allow maximum flexibility. You can pick an individual lesson or cluster of lessons in order to feature a certain author or literary selection. Or, you may want to concentrate on a particular area of critical reading. In either case, the *Daybooks*, like *Write Source 2000*, allow you to pick up the book and use it for days or weeks at a time, then leave it, perhaps to teach a novel or longer writing project, and then return to it again later in the semester. You, not the text, set the classroom agenda.

Another similarity between the *Daybooks* and the *Write Source 2000* handbook lies in the approach to writing. Both begin from the premise that writing is, first and foremost, a means of discovery. "Writing to learn" is the common expression for this idea. Only by expression can we discover what lies within us. *Write Source 2000* introduces this idea in its opening chapter, and the *Daybooks*, by promoting daily writing, give you the tool to make writing a consistent, regular feature of your classes.

But the *Daybooks* only start students on a daily course of reading and writing. Individual writing assignments are initiated but not carried through to final drafts. The purpose of writing in the *Daybooks* is mostly one of discovery, creative expression, clarification of ideas or interpretations, and idea generation. The *Daybooks* are intended to be starting points, places to ruminate and organize thoughts about literature, as opposed to offering definitive instructions about how to craft an essay or write a persuasive letter. That's where *Write Source 2000* comes in. It picks up where the *Daybooks* leave off, providing everything students need to create a polished essay or literary work.

The accompanying chart correlates writing assignments in the *Daybooks* to *Write Source 2000*.

Daybook Lesson	Writing Activity	*Write Source 2000* reference
Angles of Literacy		
1. Becoming an Active Reader	react to a story	175-181, 345
2. Story Connections	write a journal entry	48, 145-148
3. An Author's Perspective	write about a story	175-179, 345
4. Language and Craft	describe an author's craft	175-179
5. Focus on the Writer	write a paragraph	104-106, 175-181

Daybook Lesson	Writing Activity	*Write Source 2000* reference
Essentials of Reading		
1. Thinking Ahead	explain predictions	127, 285
2. Adding Things Up	write a letter	149-152
3. What's the Big Idea?	identify the main idea	310
4. In Your Opinion	write a letter to the editor	121-122, 242-250, 292-293
5. Reflecting	reflect on a poem, describe incident	126, 153-159, 196-197
Essentials of Story		
1. Time and Place	analyze setting	176, 287
2. The Cast	describe characters	176
3. The Vantage Point	rewrite part of a story	184-191, 344
4. The Framework	summarize the plot	176, 214-216
5. The Message	retitle a story	191
Story and Genre		
1. An Outside Perspective	react to a story	175-181, 345
2. In His Own Words	write a news article	165-174, 313
3. Another Perspective	write about nonfiction	285, 287
4. A Poetic Portrait	write a poem	198-207
5. Thinking About Genres	create a collage	288
The Art of Language		
1. Show, Don't Tell	write a poem	198-207
2. Conveying Feelings	create a collage	288
3. Making Comparisons	write a poem	139, 198-207
4. Another Way to Compare	write a character sketch	123, 188
5. Symbols	draw a picture	
The Art of Argument		
1. Thinking About Thesis	record actions	209-212
2. Supporting Your Thesis	plan an argument	118-122, 292-296
3. Using Facts and Statistics	identify sources	55, 262-264
4. Refute Opposition	refute opposing arguments	121-122, 287, 289
5. Understanding Audience	plan an argument	118-122, 292-296

Daybook Lesson	**Writing Activity**	**Write Source 2000** reference
Active Reading: Poetry		
1. What's It All Mean?	write about a poem	196-197, 286-287
2. Bringing Yourself to a Poem	answer questions	196-197, 287, 289
3. How a Poem Sounds	evaluate two forms	194-197, 289, 312
4. Sound Effects	write a poem	194-207
5. A Figure of Speech	write a poem	194-207
Active Reading: Persuasive Writing		
1. The Viewpoint	write a letter	242-245, 289
2. The Support	write a paragraph	103, 289
3. The Language	analyze a review	287, 289,
4. The Emotional Appeal	evaluate an essay	287, 289
5. The Tone	write about nonfiction	285-287
Focus on the Writer: Ray Bradbury		
1. Bradbury's Characters	write a dialogue	190, 288
2. Bradbury's Settings	draw a scene	188, 288
3. Bradbury's Plots	write about a story	175-179, 345
4. Bradbury's Themes	write about theme	143, 287-289,
5. Bradbury's World	design a book cover	53-60, 288

Angles of Literacy

by Louann Reid

When we view something of potential value, such as a diamond or an antique vase, we often examine it from all sides. We hold it up and slowly turn it, looking first at the front, then the sides and back. Combining information from each perspective, we construct a fuller picture of the object and its worth. Similarly, we can examine a concept or idea from several angles, or perspectives, using a variety of approaches to understand a complex concept. Perhaps no concept in education is more complex—or more important—than literacy.

"Literacy" is frequently defined as the ability to read and write. But people also need to be able to read critically, write effectively, draw diagrams, collaborate with others, listen carefully, and understand complex instructions. In short, literacy means being able to do whatever is required to communicate effectively in a variety of situations. Angles of Literacy is the term we use in these *Daybooks* to identify five approaches to becoming literate.

THE FIVE ANGLES

The Angles of Literacy are major perspectives from which to examine a text. Strategies within each angle further define each one. Activities in the *Daybooks* provide students with multiple opportunities to become autonomous users of the strategies on other literature that they will encounter.

The angles are listed in an order that reflects the way that readers and writers first engage with the text. They are encouraged to move gradually from that initial engagement to a more evaluative or critical stance where they study the author's language and craft, life, and work. They critique the texts they read and consider what other critics have written. Moving from engagement through interpretation to evaluation is the process that Louise Rosenblatt and later reader-response critics advocate.

In our own work with middle school and secondary school students, we have repeatedly seen the value of encouraging students to read and write using all three stages—engagement, interpretation, evaluation. We also know that students sometimes begin at a different stage in the process—perhaps with interpretation rather than engagement. So, our five angles are not meant to be a hierarchy. Students may begin their engagement with the text using any angle and proceed in any order. Depending on the text and the context, readers might start with making personal connections to the stories in an essay. If the text is by an author that the students know well, they might naturally begin by comparing this work to the author's other works.

STRATEGIES

Strategies are plans or approaches to learning. By using some strategies over and over, students can learn to comprehend any text. The *Daybook* activities, such as annotating or visualizing a specific poem, story, or essay, provide students multiple opportunities to develop these strategies. From using this scaffolding students gradually become more independent readers and, ultimately, fully literate.

Because strategies are employed through activities, it may seem at first that they are the same thing. Yet, it is important to remember that a strategy is a purposeful plan. When, as readers, we select a strategy such as underlining key phrases, we have selected this action deliberately to help us differentiate between important information and unimportant information. We may use a double-entry log (an activity) to identify the metaphors in a poem. Our purpose in doing so is to understand figurative language (a strategy).

At the end of each lesson, the strategies are explicitly stated. In a sentence or two, the main point of the activity is noted. When students complete all 70 lessons in a *Daybook*, they will have 70 statements of what they, as active readers, can do to read critically and write effectively.

Reflection is a vital component in helping students understand the use of strategies. After using a particular strategy, students need to step back and consider whether the strategy worked or did not work. They might think about how an approach or a strategy can change their understanding of what they read and write. Students might ask themselves a series of questions such as: What have I done? What have I learned? What would I do differently next time? How did the angle or strategy affect my understanding? What would I understand differently if I had changed the angle or the strategy?

ACTIVITIES

Each lesson in these *Daybooks* contains activities for students. From rereading to discussing with a partner to making a story chart, students learn how to become more critical readers and more effective writers. Many activities encourage students to write to learn. Other activities encourage students to increase their understanding of a text by visualizing it in a sketch or a graphic organizer. But, as much as possible, the *Daybooks* try to encourage students to make a creative written response with a poem, some dialogue, a character sketch, or some other creative assignment.

We have selected activities that work particularly well with the texts in the lesson and with the strategies we want students to develop. However, as you will see when you and your students use the *Daybooks*, there are several possible activities that could reinforce a particular strategy. You may want to have students try some of these activities, such as making a story chart or using a double-entry log, when they read other texts in class. This would also be another opportunity to have students ask themselves the reflective questions.

Angles of Literacy

ANGLE OF VISION	STRATEGIES	SELECTED ACTIVITIES
Interacting with a Text	• underlining key phrases • writing questions or comments in the margin • noting word patterns and repetitions • circling unknown words • keeping track of the story or idea as it unfolds	• Write down initial impressions. • Re-read. • Write a summary of the poem. • Generate two questions and one "certainty." Then, discuss the questions and statement in a small group.
Making Connections to the Stories within a Text	• paying attention to the stories being told • connecting the stories to one's own experience • speculating on the meaning or significance of incidents	• Make a story chart with three columns—incident in the poem, significance of the incident, related incident in my life. • Write a news story of events behind the story in the poem.
Shifting Perspectives	• examining the author's viewpoint • analyzing arguments • evaluating persuasive techniques • forming interpretations • comparing texts	• Discuss with a partner or small group how you might read a poem differently if: 　the speaker were female 　you believe the speaker is a parent • Rewrite the text from a different point of view.
Studying the Language and Craft of a Text	• understanding figurative language • looking at the way the author uses words • modeling the style of other writers • studying various kinds of literature	• Use a double-entry log to identify metaphors and the qualities implied by the comparison. • Examine the title of the poem and its relationship to the text.
Focusing on the Writer's Life and Work	• reading what the author says about the writing • reading what others say • making inferences about the connections between an author's life and work • analyzing the writer's style • paying attention to repeated themes and topics in the work by one author	• Read about the poet's life. Then make an inference chart to record evidence from the poet's life, an inference, a comparison to the poem. • Write an evaluation of the poem. Then read what one or more critics have said about the poem or poet. Finally, write a short response, either agreeing or disagreeing with the critic. Support your ideas with textual evidence.

Responding to Literature Through Writing

by Ruth Vinz

We have found that students' encounters with literature are enriched when they write their way toward understanding. The writing activities in the *Daybooks* are intended to help students explore and organize their ideas and reactions during and after reading. We make use of the exploratory and clarifying roles of writing through various activities.

Exploratory assignments include those through which students question, analyze, annotate, connect, compare, personalize, emulate, map, or chart aspects in the literary selections. Generally these assignments aid students' developing interpretations and reactions to the subjects, themes, or literary devices in the literature they are reading. Other writing activities offer students the opportunity to clarify their understanding of what they've read. These assignments lead students to look at other perspectives, determine the significance of what they read, and prioritize, interpret, question, and reflect on initial impressions. Further, students are asked to create literature of their own as a way of applying the concepts they're learning. Writing to clarify also involves students in reflection, where they are asked to think about their reactions and working hypotheses. Taken together, the writing activities represent a series of strategies that students can apply to the complex task of reading literature.

The writing activities included in the *Daybooks* start students on the path toward understanding. We did not take it as the function of the writing activities in this book to lead students through the writing process toward final, finished drafts. Although examples of extensions are included here in the Teacher's Guide, the writing in the *Daybooks* introduces first draft assignments that may lead into more formal writing if you, as the teacher, so choose.

You will have your own ideas about assisting students with the writing activities or extending the writing beyond the *Daybooks*. We think it's important for you to remind students that the writing in which they engage is useful for their reading outside the *Daybooks*. For example, students may use various types of maps, charts, or diagrams introduced in the *Daybooks* when they read a novel. They may find that the response notes become a strategy they use regularly. Once exposed to imitation and modeling, students may find these useful tools for understanding an author's style, language, or structure. If your students develop a conscious awareness of the strategies behind the particular writing activities, they can apply these in other reading situations.

Writing assignments to explore and to clarify students' developing interpretations are incorporated in two types of activities, both of which are elaborated on below.

WRITING ABOUT LITERATURE

You will find activities in every cluster of lessons that call upon students to write about the literature they are reading. We developed these writing assignments to help facilitate, stimulate, support, and shape students' encounters with literature. We think the assignments have four purposes:

(1) to connect the literature to the students' personal experiences; (2) to re-examine the text for various purposes (language and craft, connections with other texts, shifting perspectives, developing interpretations); (3) to develop hypotheses, judgments, and critical interpretations; (4) to apply the idea behind the lesson to a new literary text or situation.

The types of writing we have used to fulfill these purposes are:

1. Response Notes

Students keep track of their initial responses to the literature by questioning, annotating, and marking up the text in various ways. The response notes are used to get students in the habit of recording what they are thinking while reading. Many times we circle back and ask them to build on what they have written with a particular focus or way of responding. In the response notes, students are encouraged to make personal connections, re-examine text, jot down ideas for their own writing, and monitor their changing responses.

2. Personal Narrative

Students write personal stories that connect or relate to what they have read. In some cases, the narratives tell the stories of students' prior reading experiences or how a literary selection relates to their life experiences. Other activities use personal narrative to apply and refine students' understanding of narrative principles.

3. Idea Fund

Students collect ideas for writing—catalogs, lists, charts, clusters, diagrams, double-entry logs, sketches, or maps. These forms of idea gathering are useful for analyzing particular literary selections and will aid the initial preparation for longer pieces of critical analysis.

4. Short Response

Students write summaries; paraphrase main themes or ideas; and compose paragraphs of description, exposition, explanation, evaluation, and interpretation.

5. Analysis

Students write short analyses that take them beyond summarizing the literary selection or their personal reactions to it. The analytic activities engage students in recognizing symbols and figures of speech and the links between events, characters, or images. Again, these short analytical responses are intended to prepare students for longer, critical interpretation that you, as a teacher, might assign.

6. Speculation

Students' speculations are encouraged by writing activities that engage them in predicting, inferring, and imagining. "What if . . .," "How might . . .," and "Imagine that . . ." are all ways in which students are invited to see further possibilities in the literature they read.

Students use writing to record and reflect on their reactions and interpretations. At times, students are asked to share their writing with others. Such sharing is another form of reflection through which students have an opportunity to "see again" their own work in the context of what others have produced.

The writing activities in the *Daybooks* will help students connect what they read with what they experience and with what they write, and also to make connections between the literary selections and literary techniques. The activities encourage students to experiment with a range of forms, choose a range of focuses, and reflect on what they have learned from these. We hope the writing serves to give students access to a kind of literary experience they can value and apply in their future reading

WRITING LITERATURE

Within a literary work, readers find a writer's vision, but readers also co-create the vision along with the writer and learn from his or her craft. We've asked our students to write literature of their own as a way of responding to what they read. Through writing literature, students can explore facets of the original work or use the techniques of a variety of authors. Here are a number of the activities introduced in the *Daybooks*:

1. Take the role of writer

Students write imaginative reconstructions of gaps in a text by adding another episode, adding dialogue, rewriting the ending, adding a section before or after the original text, adding characters, or changing the setting. Such imaginative entries into the text require that students apply their knowledge of the original.

2. Imitation and Modeling

The idea of modeling and imitation is not new. Writers learn from other writers. The modeling activities are intended to help students "read like a writer." In these activities, students experiment with nuances of expression, syntactic and other structural principles, and apply their knowledge of literary devices (for example, *rhythm, imagery, metaphor*). One goal in educating students with literature is to make explicit what writers do. One way to achieve the goal is to provide models that illustrate various principles of construction.

3. Original Pieces

Students write poems, character sketches, monologues, dialogues, episodes, vignettes, and descriptions as a way to apply the knowledge about language and craft they are gaining through their reading.

4. Living Others' Perspectives

Writing from others' viewpoints encourages students to step beyond self to imagine other perspectives. Students write from a character's point of view, compose diary entries or letters, explain others' positions or opinions, and other reactions to a situation. These writing activities encourage students to explore the concerns of others and to project other perspectives through their writing.

The writing becomes a record of students' developing and changing ideas about literature. By the time students have finished all of the writing in this book, they will have used writing strategies that can assist them in all future reading.

Reading, Writing, and Assessment

by Fran Claggett

As teachers, we all cope with the complexities of assessing student performance. We must be careful readers of student work, attentive observers of student participation in various activities, and focused writers in responding to student work. We must understand the value of rewarding what students do well and encouraging them to improve. Above all, we need to make the criteria for assessment clear to students.

THE DAYBOOKS

The *Daybooks* provide visible accounts of many aspects of the reading process. Students record all the various permutations of active reading and writing. In the current view of most teachers and researchers, reading is a process of constructing meaning through transactions with a text. In this view, the individual reader assumes responsibility for interpreting a text guided not only by the language of the text but also by the associations, cultural experiences, and prior knowledge that the reader brings to the interpretive task. Meaning does not reside solely within the words on the page. Our view of reading emphasizes the role of the reader. Construction of meaning, rather than the gaining and displaying of knowledge should be the goal of reading instruction. This rule is reflected throughout the *Daybooks*, which guide students in how to read, respond to, interpret, and reflect on carefully selected works of literature.

Within these lessons, students interact with a text from five angles of literacy. The *Daybooks* make it possible for both students and teachers to track students' increasing sophistication in using the angles to make sense of their reading. Through the strategies presented in the lessons, students learn to express their understanding of a text. They will do such things as show their understanding of figurative language and the importance of form; write about how characters are developed and change; and demonstrate their understanding of how a piece of literature develops.

THE ROLE OF THE TEACHER

The teacher is critical to the *Daybook* agenda. Conceivably, a teacher could pass out the *Daybooks* and turn the students loose, but that would not result in the carefully guided reading and writing that is intended. Rather, the teachers are central to student success. Because of the format of the *Daybooks*, lessons are short, each taking no more than a normal class period. They are intended to be complete in themselves, yet most teachers will see that there are numerous opportunities for extensions, elaborations, further readings, group work, and writing. The Teacher's Guide provides some suggestions; you will think of many others. The *Daybooks* offer guidelines for reading and thinking, for writing and drawing used in the service of reading. They also provide many opportunities for students to write pieces of their own, modeling, responding, interpreting, and reflecting on the pieces that they have read. Many of these pieces might lead to later revision, refining, group response, and editing. It is the teacher, however, who knows the students well enough to see which pieces would be worthwhile to work with and which it is best to leave as exercises rather than completed works.

In assessing the *Daybooks*, it is important to remember to look at the students' growing facility with the processes of reading. As is true with all learning, there will be false starts, abandoned practices, and frustrations, yet also illuminations, progress, and occasional epiphanies. No music teacher ever graded every attempt at mastering a piece of music. We, too, must resist the urge—honed by years of assessing only products or finished papers—of overassessing the *Daybooks*. We must consider them the place where students are free to think things through, change their minds, even start over. But you can be alert to what the student is doing well, what is frustrating, what needs more time. To that end, we have provided a chart which may be useful in getting a sense of how students are progressing in using angles of literacy. By duplicating the chart for each student, you can track progress through the lessons. We would like to encourage the idea of jotting down notations as you work with students during the class period or look over the *Daybooks* after class. In this way, you can amass a sizable amount of information over a grading period. Coupled with a student self-assessment, you will have tangible evidence of achievement in the *Daybooks*.

INDIVIDUAL STUDENT EIGHT-WEEK ASSESSMENT CHART

The columns for each week's lessons can be used in different ways. We suggest the number system: a 5 for insightful, imaginative thinking or responding, a 1 for a minimal attempt. Some teachers prefer the check, check-plus, check-minus system. There is even room, if you turn the chart sideways, to make some notations.

Angles of Literacy

INTERACTING WITH A TEXT	I	II	III	IV	V	VI	VII	VIII
The student demonstrates understanding by using interactive strategies such as:								
underlining key phrases								
writing questions or comments in the margin								
noting word patterns and repetitions								
circling unknown words								
keeping track of ideas as they unfold								

MAKING CONNECTIONS	I	II	III	IV	V	VI	VII	VIII
The student makes connections to the stories in a text by:								
paying attention to the stories in the text								
connecting ideas and themes in the text to personal ideas, experience, feelings, and knowledge								
making connections to other texts, movies, television shows, or other media								

SHIFTING PERSPECTIVES	I	II	III	IV	V	VI	VII	VIII
The student is able to shift perspectives to examine a text from many angles. When prompted, the student will engage in such strategies as these:								
examining the author's viewpoint								
analyzing arguments								
evaluating persuasive techniques								
comparing texts								

STUDYING THE LANGUAGE AND CRAFT OF A TEXT

	I	II	III	IV	V	VI	VII	VIII

The student will demonstrate an understanding of the way language and craft operate in a text. Specifically, the student will:

show how imagery, metaphor, and figurative language are central to literature

demonstrate an understanding of how an author's vocabulary and use of language are integral to the overall work

use modeling to demonstrate an understanding of style and form

demonstrate understanding of various genres and forms of literature

FOCUSING ON THE WRITER

	I	II	III	IV	V	VI	VII	VIII

The student will demonstrate a rich understanding of a single writer's work, including:

interpreting short texts by the author

making inferences about the connections between an author's life and work

analyzing the writer's style

drawing conclusions about repeated themes and topics in an author's work

evaluating a text or comparing works by the same author

ANGLES OF LITERACY

Unit Overview

This unit invites students to become actively engaged in their reading through a variety of reading response methods, including marking a text, making personal connections, activating prior knowledge, learning what critics write about an author, and connecting an autobiographical excerpt to the fiction and poetry of an author. Students will explore writings by Gary Soto as they practice these strategies.

Literature Focus

	Lesson	Literature
1.	Becoming an Active Reader	**Gary Soto,** from *A Summer Life* (Autobiography)
		Gary Soto, from "Seventh Grade" (Short Story)
2.	Story Connections	**Gary Soto,** from "Seventh Grade" (Short Story)
3.	An Author's Perspective	**Gary Soto,** from "Seventh Grade" (Short Story)
4.	Language and Craft	**Gary Soto,** "Oranges" (Poetry)
5.	Focus on the Writer	**Gary Soto,** from *Living Up the Street* (Autobiography)

Reading Focus

1. Active readers get involved in their reading by marking selections with their own ideas, questions, and comments.
2. When you connect your reading with your own experiences, you can get new insights about your reading and about yourself.
3. Noticing an author's perspective helps you to understand the author's messages.
4. Active readers pay close attention to the way authors use words and sentences.
5. Knowing the story of an author's life can give you insights into his or her writing.

Writing Focus

1. Do a quickwrite response to explore questions about the author.
2. Write about a memory in a journal entry.
3. Analyze the elements of Gary Soto's perspective in a short story.
4. Create book jacket copy focusing on the craft of the writer.
5. Explain your feelings about Gary Soto and his work.

One Becoming an Active Reader

Critical Reading

FOCUS
Make a selection "your own" by marking up a text.

BACKGROUND
Gary Soto is poet, short story writer, and essayist who focuses often on his own childhood in the barrio of Fresno, California. In his short story, "Seventh Grade," Soto brings these memories to the language which he uses: "They shook hands, *raza*-style, and jerked their heads at one another in a *saludo de vato*." The text humorously reveals the device that the seventh grade boys, especially protagonist Victor and his friend Michael, use to attract girls in their school.

➤ This lesson introduces students to techniques of active reading. Its purpose is to get students started in physically marking up a text. Encourage students to write questions, comments, and observations as they read. This helps them to connect actively with the text, rather than be passive. Because some students highlight everything as they read, you may need to explain that effective readers need to be more discriminating.

FOR DISCUSSION AND REFLECTION
➤ What reasons does Victor have for taking French as his elective? (He wants someday to travel to France where there are rivers, huge churches, and fair-skinned people. Also, Teresa, the girl he is interested in, plans to take French. It is a language he does not know.)

➤ What method for impressing girls have both Michael and Victor adopted? (Like the male models in *GQ* magazine, they scowl all the time. They think girls are noticing them.)

➤ What questions did you have about this selection? (Answers will vary.)

Writing

QUICK ASSESS
Do students' free writes:

✓ include specific impressions of the author based on the story excerpt?

✓ offer personal, first-person response?

Students should review all of their notes and then share their seventh grade memories with their classmates. As students explain their feelings about Gary Soto, ask them to think about why they like or dislike his writing so far.

READING AND WRITING EXTENSIONS
➤ Encourage students to read another selection by Gary Soto from *Local News*, a collection of thirteen short stories, and to write a review of one for the class.

➤ "Eleven," by Sandra Cisneros, in *Women Hollering Creek,* depicts a young Latina girl's feeling about turning eleven. After reading it to students, have each of them write a paragraph about a memory associated with a particular age or grade level.

Two Story Connections

C r i t i c a l   R e a d i n g

FOCUS
Relating what you read to your own experiences helps you get actively involved in the text.

BACKGROUND
In this lesson, "Seventh Grade," by Gary Soto, continues. Victor tries to make contact with Teresa by lingering in homeroom and finding her at lunch break. He does manage to earn a smile before going to their common class, French.

➤ Prior knowledge and experience are important aspects of reading comprehension. Help students try to connect information in the story with their own experiences. As students read this section of the story, they should jot down memories and associations. (For example, I remember when I was embarrassed like that; math is a hard subject for me, too; I can remember feeling left out when I was not part of a group, and so on.)

FOR DISCUSSION AND REFLECTION
➤ Why was Victor's first face-to-face encounter with Teresa unsuccessful? (Although he planned to run into her when she exited homeroom, he didn't say anything clever. When she said, "Hi, Victor," he replied, "Yeah, that's me.")

➤ Has Victor been able to hide his crush on Teresa? (No, he blurts her name out in English as an example of a noun. Next, another student picks up on it and gives Teresa's house as an example of a place noun. All the other kids giggle.)

➤ What parts of Victor's story can you connect with? (Students might connect with having a crush on someone or acting silly in order to get noticed.)

W r i t i n g

QUICK ASSESS
Do students' journal entries:

✔ provide a detailed account of a memory?

✔ include personal feeling?

Before they write a journal entry, review with students the elements of a journal and write these on the board: uses *I*, usually written on a daily basis or in reaction to a particular event, not a menu list of everything that happens in a day like a schedule, offers feelings about the event, and so on.

READING AND WRITING EXTENSIONS
➤ Have students read from another diary—*The Diary of Latoya Hunter*, an actual diary of a seventh grade girl first written as a school assignment; *Zlata's Diary*, a vivid account of a young girl living in war-torn Bosnia; or the humorous *The Secret Diary of Adrian Mole*, about a teenager in Britain. Ask them to share any personal connections they made.

➤ Encourage students to maintain a writer's notebook—a combination of journal entries, favorite quotations and poetry, and small mementoes from and about special places. The notebook will become a resource for future writing.

Three An Author's Perspective

Critical Reading

FOCUS

Understanding an author's perspective can help you make sense of his or her writing.

BACKGROUND

Lesson Three looks at how the background of any author is often evident in his or her writing. While readers may actively engage through personal response and by making connections to their background, it is important to see how much of an author's own life comes through in his or her writing. This is the writer's perspective.

➤ The three passages about Gary Soto indicate that he is interested in writing about his youth and in focusing on everyday details of his California childhood in Fresno. The Hispanic population of the area is nearly 25 percent. It clearly shapes Soto's interests and perspective. If students recognize an author's perspective, they will be able to understand more clearly why he or she includes certain details and events.

FOR DISCUSSION AND REFLECTION

➤ What does Soto mean when he says, "The rosebushes of shame on his face became bouquets of love"? (Earlier, in French class, Victor blushed with embarrassment, but now he is happy and hopeful.)

➤ What are some of the "human feelings" Soto tries to capture in his writing to which readers can connect? (Answers will vary, but they may include the envy of the rich, the loneliness of having no girlfriend or boyfriend, fear and boredom, embarrassment in front of peers, and so on.)

Writing

QUICK ASSESS

Do students' responses:

✓ clearly focus on one element of Soto's perspective?

✓ use specific supporting evidence from the story?

Before students write about the story, list the four elements of Soto's perspective on the board and brainstorm with the class details from "Seventh Grade" that connect to one or more of the categories. (The youthful quality could be the boys imitating models from magazines to look cool. The upbeat approach could be Victor thinking that he is going to like seventh grade. Young people's emotions are reflected in Victor's embarrassment in both math and French class. Commonplace details are evident in Soto's description of the cafeteria lunch and the daily schedule of a seventh grader.)

READING AND WRITING EXTENSIONS

➤ Encourage students to conduct an "author study" on a writer whose work they enjoy. Have them share connections they found between the author's life and one or more pieces of writing.

➤ Ask students to read another story by Gary Soto and report orally on whether they recognized in that work any of the elements described in this lesson.

See also Answer Key, page 112

Four Language and Craft

Critical Reading

FOCUS

Gary Soto paints the resolution of the poem:

"I peeled my orange / That was so bright against / The gray of December / That, from some distance, / Someone might have thought / I was making a fire in my hands."

BACKGROUND

Gary Soto's poetry reflects another dimension of his writing talent. Joyce Carol Oates praised Soto's poetry, explaining that his "poems are fast, funny, heartrending, and achingly believable, like Polaroid love letters, or snatches of music heard out of a passing car; patches of beauty like patches of the sunlight; the very pulse of life."

➤ "Oranges" relates the story of a twelve-year-old boy and the first time he walks a girl home. The underlying message of poverty is in the poem since the girl selected a candy for a dime, and the boy had only a nickel and an orange to give to the female store owner, who does accept it. Her action speaks to kindness and caring between people.

➤ To help students respond in the margins of the poem by underlining important words and ideas, cue them to look for strong images ("Cold, and weighted down / With two oranges in my jacket"), vivid descriptions of feelings ("Light in her eyes, a smile / Starting at the corners / Of her mouth."), and pacing for suspense ("When I looked up, / The lady's eyes met mine, / And held them, knowing / Very well what it was all / About").

FOR DISCUSSION AND REFLECTION

➤ What are some of the images Soto uses to describe the setting in the poem? (Some clues include a used car lot, a line of newly planted trees, a drugstore, a house with a porch.)

➤ What is it that the boy feels that the drugstore owner understands? (The woman realized the boy did not have the necessary money when he placed the orange on the counter. She also recognized how important it was for him to be able to buy the candy for the girl.)

➤ Do you see any connections between "Oranges" and "Seventh Grade"? (Responses will vary. In both, adults understand that a boy is trying to impress a girl and, thus, do not cause further embarrassment.)

Writing

QUICK ASSESS

Do students' book jacket blurbs:

✓ contain author and title names?

✓ reflect creativity?

Encourage students to develop book jacket copy that includes specific details about Soto's writing based on the comparison chart, perhaps using phrases that might have been stated by a critic.

READING AND WRITING EXTENSIONS

➤ Have students use pictures, images, clip art, or photographs to visually extend their responses to Soto's writings. Can they take one of the ideas from the chart and translate it into a picture?

➤ Have students write a book review for the inside flap of their book jacket. Remind them that this usually is a summary of the story with a recommendation to particular readers.

Five Focus on the Writer

Critical Reading

FOCUS

The beauty of Gary Soto's writing comes through even when he describes grueling work:

"I poured them on the paper tray, which was bordered by a wooden frame that kept the grapes from rolling off, and they spilled like jewels from a pirate's chest."

BACKGROUND

Memoir is a form of autobiographical writing that focuses on important events in a person's life, rather than a sequential retelling of the person's years. It is a first-person account of events, so feelings are often expressed along with the factual retelling of the experiences.

➤ The excerpt from Gary Soto's *Living Up the Street* gives a picture of the grueling work of grape pickers in California. Soto may be representative of many young people as he harvests grapes with his mother to earn money for new school clothes. He soon realizes how difficult it is to accumulate money at six cents a tray. A day's work might earn him four dollars.

➤ As students read, encourage them to mark points that reveal Soto's feelings and background.

FOR DISCUSSION AND REFLECTION

➤ How does Soto's mother motivate him to continue to work? (She talks about his new school and how Rick and Debra will be sorry because they will have no new clothes for school.)

➤ How does Soto motivate himself to continue the work? (Answers may include daydreaming about diving into water and loving it, baseball, would-be girlfriends, singing.)

➤ Does this motivation work? (Barely. Soto realizes that eight hours of work only nets him four dollars to spend.)

Writing

QUICK ASSESS

Do students' explanations:

✓ express a clear opinion?

✓ use supporting details from the three readings?

After identifying autobiographical details from "Seventh Grade" and "Oranges," students express their personal response to the writing of Gary Soto. While their response offers opinion, remind students to include details from different pieces to support what they think.

READING AND WRITING EXTENSIONS

➤ Gary Soto recounts an episode when a mother tries to tell about "when I was a child." Ask students to think of a time when older relatives or friends tried to convince them that things were so much harder in the past. Have them share their memories with classmates.

➤ Ask students to develop a questionnaire for an older person—a friend, a relative, or neighbor—to answer. Suggest that they focus on one aspect of life: work, education, schooling, or leisure activities. Have the respondents answer the questions in terms of what life was like when they were twelve and encourage students to share their findings with the class.

See also Answer Key, page 112-113

Unit Overview

This unit aims at strengthening students' reading comprehension skills by making them more aware of strategies that good readers employ. As they read a variety of nonfiction, students will develop their abilities to offer predictions, make inferences, decide on a thesis in nonfiction, and evaluate and reflect on what they have read.

Literature Focus

	Lesson	Literature
1.	Thinking Ahead	**Latoya Hunter,** from *The Diary of Latoya Hunter* (Nonfiction)
2.	Adding Things Up	
3.	What's the Big Idea?	**Kendall Hamilton and Patricia King,** "Playgrounds of the Future" (Nonfiction)
4.	In Your Opinion	
5.	Reflecting	**Robert Frost,** "A Time to Talk" (Poetry)

Reading Focus

1. Making predictions and checking them helps you get more out of your reading.
2. Making inferences can deepen your insights into your reading.
3. Identifying the main idea helps you to clarify what the selection is all about.
4. Evaluating helps you think critically about what you read.
5. Reflection can help you to better understand your reading and yourself.

Writing Focus

1. Explain your reasons for making predictions about a diary entry.
2. Write a letter that describes the author.
3. Identify the topic and main idea of a nonfiction piece.
4. Compose a letter to the editor evaluating an article.
5. Reflect on and respond to a poem.

One Thinking Ahead

Critical Reading

FOCUS

From *The Diary of Latoya Hunter:*

"Well Diary, what I assume was the worst week of J.H. is over. I hope things will get better next week. It has to. It can't get any worse…or can it?"

BACKGROUND

At the end of one school year at PS 94 in the Bronx, teacher Robert Pelka wrote in the *New York Times* that a graduating sixth grader, Latoya Hunter, had an "incredible writing talent." Intrigued, editor Richard Marek contacted Latoya and asked her if she would like to maintain a diary for the next school year. She agreed, and her ten-month diary was later published. Unlike some of the diaries that students read in middle school, Latoya is not struggling with world problems. She gives a personal account of a year in seventh grade.

➤ Lesson One introduces students to the important reading strategy of prediction. Active readers are constantly taking in information and making guesses about what will follow. Weak readers need to be made aware of this strategy. They also need to see that sensible predictions are based on information that the text gives them or that they infer.

FOR DISCUSSION AND REFLECTION

➤ Why does Latoya believe she will be targeted as a victim of Freshman Day? (She feels she is one of the types: a quiet one, one not in the crowd, one who doesn't act like an animal "on the street.")

➤ Which words show that Latoya might be exaggerating what will happen on Freshman Day? ("deranged minds of the 8th and 9th graders," "attack kids in the hall," "dead-in-an-alley-headed crowd," something "snapped in the minds of the older kids")

Writing

QUICK ASSESS

Do students' responses:

✔ express their predictions clearly?

✔ give specific reasons for these guesses?

Before students write about their predictions, model an example of a prediction with a reason behind it. For example, a reader could predict that Latoya will stay home on Freshman Day. This could be based on the quotation, "Is it strange for someone to *want* to get sick so they can't leave their house for a day?" Invite students to review their predictions, locating quotations as support.

READING AND WRITING EXTENSIONS

➤ To practice prediction skills, have students read the short story "The Open Window" by Saki. Ask them to pause after every couple of paragraphs and share their thoughts about what will happen next.

➤ Ask students to maintain a diary for two weeks as a homework assignment. Have them focus on school events and their feelings, rather than on hourly accounts of the day.

See also Answer Key, page 113

TWO Adding Things Up

Critical Reading

FOCUS
Effective readers know how to "read between the lines":

"I can't believe I'm here writing to you with no scratches or bruises. I actually made it."

BACKGROUND
Inferential comprehension, a higher level of reading in which readers go beyond the literal text and "read between the lines," may seem difficult to some young readers. Explain that it is like detective work, where a reader needs to put clues together to get to a conclusion.

➤ In "Adding Things Up," students reread the same section of the diary as in Lesson One. However, they are to figure out what they know about the characteristics and interests of Latoya from what she has written. For example, they might infer that she may exaggerate the upcoming Freshman Day: "I've heard rumors that they attack kids in the hall. . . . I feel there will be a lot of fights between the freshmen and seniors." Or they might infer that she categorizes students at J.H.S. 80: "I'm not about to change to fit in their dead-in-an-alley-headed crowd" or "I witnessed one of them with a geeky looking boy . . . ."

FOR DISCUSSION AND REFLECTION
➤ How aware are the school officials of the threats of Freshman Day? (Students will likely say that they are very aware, since the principal had warned that anyone who touched a freshman would be suspended.)

➤ What can you infer about Latoya from her concern about Freshman Day? (She is not overly confident of herself and worries how she fits in.)

Writing

QUICK ASSESS
Do students' letters:

✓ follow the format of a friendly letter?

✓ incorporate quotations for support?

✓ make appropriate inferences?

Before they begin their letters describing Latoya, have students refer to response notes that show what is important about school for her. For example, Latoya could be seen as someone interested in making a mark at the junior high: "I intend to make something of myself." Then have students share these ideas aloud to brainstorm a master list for the entire class. After reviewing the format for a friendly letter, students will write one to a classmate describing what they know about Latoya.

READING AND WRITING EXTENSIONS
➤ Encourage students to read the entire diary by Latoya Hunter and share their reactions to it with the class.

➤ Have students write an anonymous diary entry of at least one page. Collect and distribute these, keeping the authors unknown. Tape the entries to a wall. Have students read the entries and think about which classmate could be the author of each. After group discussion, have the real author claim his or her entry.

Three What's the Big Idea?

Critical Reading

FOCUS

Identifying the main idea or central meaning of a piece of nonfiction is essential.

BACKGROUND

While the underlying meaning in fiction is the theme, in nonfiction it is the main idea, or (sometimes) the thesis. A thesis is more than a topic in expository writing; it is the writer's opinion on the topic. While the subject or topic of nonfiction is explicit, often the thesis or message must be inferred. Other times, the writer has argued directly for his or her opinion and given many examples to support it.

➤ This lesson turns to a nonfiction piece, "Playgrounds of the Future." In many modern play areas, much of the traditional equipment of a playground—including monkey bars, merry-go-rounds, and seesaws—have been eliminated or altered for child safety. While opponents of the modifications state that these safety precautions are not really necessary—just a convenience for working parents—the writers of the article, Hamilton and King, argue that California is adopting these changes to eliminate one of the "five greatest hazards to children in the nation . . . up there with chain saws and ladders."

FOR DISCUSSION AND REFLECTION

➤ What real hazards for children in the traditional playgrounds do the writers mention? (Answers may include getting sick on the merry-go-rounds, getting trapped under apparatus, hard landings, and burned fingers.)

➤ What arguments do opponents give for these modifications? (Possible answers are that they grew up with these and are fine, that there is a lack of parental guidance at the playgrounds, that kids need to "bang against hard things.")

➤ How do you find the main idea of a piece of nonfiction? (Suggest that students decide what the author has to say about the subject.)

Writing

QUICK ASSESS

Do students' statements:

✓ reflect understanding of the article?

✓ identify the main idea?

To help students identify topic and main idea, have students work in small groups to list the pros and cons of the argument and compose a thesis statement, a combination of the topic and the point that the writers make about the topic. Copy all of the thesis statements on the board or on an overhead.

READING AND WRITING EXTENSIONS

➤ Bring in the editorial page of a major newspaper or magazine. Working in pairs, have students decide on the topic and argument within one editorial. Suggest that they try to develop several arguments against the opinion of the writer.

➤ Invite students to develop a survey to use in a nearby elementary school regarding the safety of the current playground. Have students, staff, recess monitors, and parents complete the survey. Then encourage students to tabulate the results and present a summary to the elementary school's principal.

See also Answer Key, page 113

Four In Your Opinion

C r i t i c a l   R e a d i n g

FOCUS

Evaluation of a thesis requires a discerning reader who can think about how well-supported the main idea is.

BACKGROUND

Evaluating involves giving a personal assessment of an idea or issue. In this lesson students are evaluating the thesis presented in "Playgrounds of the Future." To do this with depth of understanding, students need to reread the article responding to the text with a D for disagree or A for agree with the point. For example, ask students if they have ever been hurt at a playground. Does this personal experience influence them to agree with the writers? Or can they see that something unrelated to the equipment, like a pushy friend, might have contributed to their injury? Help students see that a critical reader needs to consider carefully what are facts and what are opinions.

FOR DISCUSSION AND REFLECTION

➤ What are the reasons given for the change to the new playground? (Possible answers include the number of injuries and fatalities, the high cost for safeguarding a traditional playground, and the threat of parental lawsuits for injuries.)

➤ Why do some people favor the playgrounds of old? (Possible answers include that safety features will create "plastic-bubble childhoods for kids," that parents are too busy to watch their kids, and that traditional playgrounds are more fun.)

W r i t i n g

QUICK ASSESS

Do students' letters:

✔ clearly explain their views of the argument?

✔ give specifics from the article as support?

✔ follow appropriate letter format?

Bring in letters to the editor from magazines and work as a group to uncover the format. Then have students "take a stand" on the issue of playgrounds for the future. In their letters to the editor of *Newsweek*, direct students to voice their opinion on the topic. While they can agree with the arguments given in the article, encourage them to add more, too.

READING AND WRITING EXTENSIONS

➤ Have students research a problem that could be a safety hazard in the middle school—for example, crowded lines to the cafeteria, bus routes, running in the halls, and so on. In a letter to the editor for the school newspaper, ask them to take a stand on the issue and offer suggestions for improvement.

➤ Invite students to create a three-panel brochure for FUTURE PLAY, INC., a company advertising a playground for the future. Include images, pictures, safety reasons, and products for the playground.

Five Reflecting

Critical Reading

FOCUS

Your responses to what you read can reveal a lot about yourself.

BACKGROUND

Robert Frost (1874–1963) was known as the "Poet of New England." The poem "A Time to Talk" comes from the anthology *Mountain Internal* (1916), which included such similar poems as "Mending Wall" and "After Apple Picking." This poetry emphasizes the simplicity of the natural world and reflects a deep understanding of human nature. "A Time to Talk" is a perfect example, blending images of farmlands of Vermont ("all the hills I haven't hoed," "mellow ground") with the importance of friendship.

➤ Lesson Five develops students' skills of reflecting as they read. Reflection means standing away from a piece of reading to determine what a reader likes or dislikes, to make a personal connection to an experience, or to make mental images of a work read. Help students to understand the process of reflection by sharing some of your own responses to this poem.

FOR DISCUSSION AND REFLECTION

➤ Does the farmer have work to be done? (Yes, he thinks of "all the hills I haven't hoed.")

➤ Why does the farmer leave his work? (He looks forward to a friendly visit, understanding that the person is more important than the work.)

➤ Have you learned anything from Frost's poem? Can you make connections to your own life? (Responses will vary.)

Writing

QUICK ASSESS

Do students' reflections:

✓ present a personal connection to the poem?

✓ show their likes and dislikes?

Help students write about a small incident in their lives that was important to them by brainstorming possibilities together—a phone call from a friend, a note pushed into a locker, a particular play in a game, and so on. Discussing how they might feel about friendship will help them think about "A Time to Talk" before they write their responses to it.

READING AND WRITING EXTENSIONS

➤ Invite students to write a "tribute poem." This is a formula poem that praises, thanks, and acknowledges the significance that a person has in the poet's life. Every other line begins, "This is for you, . . . (person's name) for . . . (add in details)." By using specific nouns, powerful adjectives, and detailed imagery, the poem becomes very personalized.

➤ Ask students to create a "Hallmark" card for a person based on a small event that was a significant moment for them. Encourage them to make pictures that recreate the feeling or the event. Have students share their cards and then display them on a wall or bulletin board.

Unit Overview

In this unit, students study basic elements of a story, including setting, mood, flat and round characters, point of view, plot, conflict, and theme. By reading and responding to excerpts from longer works by Mark Twain and Yoko Kawashima Watkins and an entire story by Mona Gardner, students deepen their understanding and appreciation of stories.

Literature Focus

	Lesson	Literature
1.	Time and Place	**Mark Twain,** from *The Adventures of Tom Sawyer* (Fiction)
2.	The Cast	**Mark Twain,** from *The Adventures of Tom Sawyer* (Fiction)
3.	The Vantage Point	**Yoko Kawashima Watkins,** from *So Far from the Bamboo Grove* (Fiction)
4.	The Framework	**Mona Gardner,** "The Dinner Party" (Short Story)
5.	The Message	

Reading Focus

1. The setting, or time and place of the action, can reflect mood or emotions in a story.
2. One way to connect with a story is to analyze its characters.
3. Point of view—the vantage point from which a story is told—helps to determine how much readers learn about each character.
4. Examining a story's plot can give you a helpful overview of the events.
5. By inferring a story's themes, you can better understand the author's ideas about life and human nature.

Writing Focus

1. Write about setting and mood.
2. Brainstorm a list of words to describe the similarities and differences between two characters.
3. Rewrite part of a story by changing the point of view.
4. Make a diagram of a story's plot.
5. Choose a new title for a story and explain its connection to the theme.

One Time and Place

Critical Reading

FOCUS

In *The Adventures of Tom Sawyer*, Twain's description of the setting helps to create the emotional atmosphere:

"They fell to thinking. A sort of undefined longing crept upon them. This took dim shape, presently—it was budding homesickness."

BACKGROUND

American writer and humorist Mark Twain—the pseudonym of Samuel Langhorne Clemens—lived from 1835–1910. *The Adventures of Tom Sawyer* provides a realistic picture of a small town on the Mississippi River, for its details come from Twain's own background in Hannibal, Missouri. His work as a steamboat pilot on the Mississippi is the origin for his pen name taken from "Mark Twain," a system for measuring the river at two fathoms deep.

➤ This lesson focuses on setting, the time and place in story. In the first excerpt, Twain uses rich description to give an idyllic playground for Tom and Huck as they begin their sojourn away from adults. The second excerpt is used to show a shift in mood, or the feeling the reader gets from the piece. Students should see that the selection of details of the setting creates the longing and homesickness: "The stillness, the solemnity that brooded in the woods, and the sense of loneliness began to tell upon the spirits of the boys."

FOR DISCUSSION AND REFLECTION

➤ What details does Twain use to show that the boys first enjoy their new environment on the Mississippi? (Answers may include "burning the bridge between them and civilization," "glad-hearted," sweet water, the reward after fishing.)

➤ What sensory details are used to describe the setting? (Some answers are "long lances of sunlight," "white sand bar," "limpid water," and a "promising nook in the riverbank.")

Writing

QUICK ASSESS

Do students' responses:

✓ incorporate details about setting?

✓ connect the setting to a mood?

Invite students to share their response notes and sketches to clarify the details of the setting. Brainstorm a list of words that can be used to describe mood (such as angry, frightened, carefree, lonely, sad) before students write a paragraph showing the change in mood from the first excerpt to the second.

READING AND WRITING EXTENSIONS

➤ Have students read Mark Twain's humorous "The Celebrated Jumping Frog of Calaveras County" and share their reactions to it with the class.

➤ Ask students to research the details of Mark Twain's life and report interesting findings to the class.

See also Answer Key, page 113

TWO The Cast

Critical Reading

FOCUS

Huckleberry Finn is one of the great and enduring characters in literature:

"In a word, everything that goes to make life precious that boy had."

BACKGROUND

Ernest Hemingway once wrote, "All modern American literature comes from one book by Mark Twain called *Huckleberry Finn* . . . it's the best we've had . . . . There was nothing before. There has been nothing so good since." The same might be said for the characterization of Huckleberry Finn, an outcast of the polite society of Hannibal, Missouri, and the idol of all of the boys in the town. With his striking use of vernacular dialect, Huckleberry is the epitome of the free spirit who is unreined by the conventions of civilization.

➤ "The Cast" presents many terms with which students can describe and think about characterization. Flat characters are those that are predictable and reliable, like a detective in a mystery story or a villain. Some of the flat characters in the novel are Tom's Aunt Polly and Huck's guardians, the Widow Douglas and her old spinster sister, Miss Watson. A reliable villain is Huck's drunken father, Pap. Three-dimensional, or round, characters are more human since they change and show different sides of their personalities. The protagonist, like Huck, occupies most of the text and often plays the role of the hero, although this is not necessary. The antagonist opposes the protagonist in action or ideas—for example, the men hunting for Jim, the slave who has run away with Huckleberry.

FOR DISCUSSION AND REFLECTION

➤ Why do you think the mothers of Hannibal dreaded Huckleberry? (Students should mention his wanton behavior and appearance. Dressed in castoff clothes, idle, lawless, and vulgar, Huck seemed wild and undisciplined, a poor role model for their children.)

➤ Why is Tom attracted to Huckleberry? (He came and went of his own free will, did not have to go to school or church, got to stay up as late as he pleased.)

Writing

QUICK ASSESS
Do students' lists:

✓ accurately reflect the characters?

✓ compare and contrast Tom and Huck?

Before students brainstorm their word lists, in small groups have students collect all of the phrases that describe the characters of Huck and Tom in this excerpt. Then have them circle those characteristics the two boys have in common—curiosity, love of adventure, use of dialect—and those that are different—Tom's structure and Huck's freedom.

READING AND WRITING EXTENSIONS

➤ Place students in literature circles to read a longer selection of the novel. Have them meet periodically to discuss the characters and ask them to sketch a major character using details from the reading.

➤ Have students pretend that they are Aunt Polly, the caretaker and adult in Tom's life. Invite them to write a lecture that Aunt Polly might give to Tom about his friendship with Huckleberry on the occasion of finding Tom with the dead cat.

See also Answer Key, page 113

Three The Vantage Point

Critical Reading

FOCUS

So Far from the Bamboo Grove uses a limited third-person point of view:

"She tasted the pepper and garlic water to show him it was safe, and the hot moisture felt good to his stomach."

BACKGROUND

Point of view is the study of the relationship between the narrator and his or her story. A first-person point of view limits what the reader knows about the other characters in the story to what the narrator thinks or says or how he or she interacts with the other characters. Authors may use this point of view in a journal or in a mystery so that the reader's information is limited to what the narrator knows. Third-person narration or point of view places the narrator as an outsider viewing the action. Sometimes the mind of only one character is given (third-person limited), and other times all characters' thoughts are revealed equally (omniscient).

➤ This lesson presents an excerpt from Watkins's *So Far from the Bamboo Grove*. As students read, they should pay attention to the thoughts and reactions of Hideyo, from whose point of view we read the story. Since it is third-person limited point of view, point out to students that we do not know the feelings of Hideyo's potential enemies, the Korean family.

FOR DISCUSSION AND REFLECTION

➤ Where do you see the feelings of Hideyo revealed in this excerpt? ("He did not know where he was or who these people were . . . . He was even fearful of being poisoned" by the woman.)

➤ Why does the family pretend the Japanese boy is a relative? (The text says, "if anyone finds out we have rescued a Japanese boy, we will be betrayed for prize money and executed.")

Writing

QUICK ASSESS

Do students' rewrites:

✓ reveal the feelings and thoughts of all of the characters?

✓ use third-person pronouns?

Before changing the point of view of the excerpt, be sure that students have underlined all of the thoughts revealed by Hideyo. Look at the words that reveal his thoughts and feelings. Give them a model of the opening line, adding the thoughts and feelings of Hee Wang—for example, "Is he a Japanese boy, Father?" asked Hee Wang, nervous that their family had stumbled upon an enemy.

READING AND WRITING EXTENSIONS

➤ Invite students to read more historical fiction novels about World War II with an adolescent as the main character. Possibilities include *The Machine Gunners* (Great Britain) by Robert Westall, *The Summer of My German Soldier* (United States) by Bette Greene, and *Lisa's War* (Scandinavia) by Carol Matas.

➤ Have students write a journal entry as if they were Hideyo remembering this first encounter with the Korean family. Remind them to use the first-person point of view to retell the episode.

See also Answer Key, page 113

Four **The Framework**

C r i t i c a l   R e a d i n g

FOCUS

Thinking about possible conflicts will help you understand a story's plot.

BACKGROUND

Lesson Four presents the plot diagram for a short story: exposition (a dinner party in India of British officers and their wives); rising action (the argument between the girl and the colonel, the American naturalist noticing the tenseness of the hostess, the milk for the cobra); climax (the American making the wager so that no one moves as he realizes the cobra is under the table); falling action (the American rushing to close the doors once the cobra escapes, the men congratulating themselves for showing more control); and resolution (Mrs. Wynnes in cool control as the cobra passes over her feet). You may want to present the diagram before the reading of the story to help in framing it.

➤ It may be wise to share with the students a little of the history of colonialism, which led the British empire to begin imperial rule over India during the nineteenth century. Because of this, many British officers and their wives were stationed in luxurious quarters of India. Of course, the role of women, at this time, was very different from what it is now; then, women had no right to vote, little work outside of the home, and most of the responsibility for social occasions.

FOR DISCUSSION AND REFLECTION

➤ What are some examples of conflict in the story? (Responses may include the male vs. the female view of how a woman would react in a crisis and the natural threat of the cobra against the dinner guests.)

➤ Who is the most observant person at the dinner party? (Students will likely say the American. He notices the strange expression of the hostess, observes the milk being put out for the cobra, and searches the rafters for the cobra.)

W r i t i n g

QUICK ASSESS

Do students' plot diagrams:

✓ include all of the events of the story?

✓ occur in chronological order?

Have students take a large sheet of chart paper to make the plot diagram for "The Dinner Party." Model the exposition first so that they understand what belongs there. Have them work in groups to plot the rest of the diagram; then post the papers around the classroom and together decide on the "best" diagram.

READING AND WRITING EXTENSIONS

➤ Have students return to an earlier story, such as Gary Soto's "Seventh Grade." Ask them to use the plot diagram to present the series of events of that story to the class.

➤ Ask students to plan a brief story using Leland Jacobs's simple formula for plots. First, they decide on the main character and what he or she wants (a new job, to win the lottery, a friend at school, and so on). Then students should decide whether the character will get what he or she wants. With that in mind, students should plan for the character to do two things to reach the goal—one that fails and one that leads to the chosen ending.

See also Answer Key, page 114

Five The Message

Critical Reading

FOCUS

Sometimes, a theme is not stated directly, and readers will need to infer it on their own.

BACKGROUND

In this lesson, students return to "The Dinner Party" to analyze it for theme, or the underlying meaning. Remind students that good cues for unlocking the theme might be to look at the lessons learned by the characters. By looking at the colonel, for example, students can find out that his opinion of women—that "a woman's unfailing reaction in any crisis . . . is to scream"—is dead wrong. By contrast, the first impulse of the American naturalist is "to jump back and warn the others, but he knows the commotion would frighten the cobra into striking." This shows that his first reaction would have been what the colonel expected for a woman. Show students that categorizing all women to act one way is disproved in the story and is probably an important message or theme.

FOR DISCUSSION AND REFLECTION

➤ Which character seems to be most judgmental of others in the story? (Students will probably say the colonel, who says that women have not outgrown the jumping-on-a-chair-at-the-sight-of-a-mouse era. The colonel also feels the American has proven him correct at the end when he has everyone remain still so the cobra could be lured out to the verandah with the milk.)

➤ What characters show restraint in the time of crisis? (Answers will be Mrs. Wynnes, since she called the servant boy for milk when she felt the cobra pass over her feet, and the American, because he wagered that all could not remain still for five minutes.)

➤ How is the story ironic? (At the beginning the colonel had said that men had more control, but Mrs. Wynnes has actually showed the most restraint by not screaming when she first felt the cobra at her feet under the table.)

Writing

QUICK ASSESS

Do students' responses:

✓ offer an appropriate title related to the theme?

✓ present a clear argument for the new title?

After listing the lessons that many characters have learned in the story, have students share these aloud before they re-title the story and explain why the new title better reflects one of the themes.

READING AND WRITING EXTENSIONS

➤ Ask students to select a story or a poem that they know has a confusing title. Ask them to bring it in for the class to read and then discuss together possible meanings.

➤ Have students research the history of the Colonial British Empire in India. Suggest that they use the Internet or encyclopedias and share details of the time period that would extend the setting of "The Dinner Party."

See also Answer Key, page 114

Unit Overview

In this unit, students will study how one subject, baseball great Jackie Robinson, can be developed through different perspectives. The genres of biography, autobiography, and poetry each develop a topic differently through the use of facts, opinions, and images. As they read about Jackie Robinson's life, students will discover for themselves the strengths and limitations of each genre.

Literature Focus

	Lesson	Literature
1.	An Outside Perspective	**Robert Peterson,** "Hero on the Ball Field" (Biography)
2.	In His Own Words	**Jackie Robinson,** from *I Never Had It Made* (Autobiography)
3.	Another Perspective	**Sharon Robinson,** from *Stealing Home* (Autobiography)
4.	A Poetic Portrait	**Lucille Clifton,** "Jackie Robinson" (Poetry)
5.	Thinking About Genres	

Reading Focus

1. When you read a biography, consider why the author has chosen to describe certain events. Ask yourself, "What do these events tell me about the subject of the biography?"

2. When you read an autobiography, consider how the writer's direct involvement might affect how he or she interprets what happened.

3. A personal account or memoir can provide readers with insights and details that may be absent from a more objective account.

4. Poets use figurative expressions and images to tell their own stories about people.

5. Different genres can provide different perspectives on the same subject. Keep in mind the strengths and limitations of each as you read.

Writing Focus

1. Complete a chart based on a biography.

2. Use a Venn diagram to compare and contrast a news article with an autobiographical excerpt.

3. Brainstorm a list of Robinson's personal characteristics based on reading selections.

4. Write an original poem about a famous person you admire.

5. Create a collage that captures the many sides of Jackie Robinson.

One An Outside Perspective

Critical Reading

FOCUS

Some biographies, such as "Hero on the Ball Field," portray their subjects in a favorable light:

"Jackie Robinson was a fiery competitor. 'This guy didn't just come to play,' an old baseball man once said. 'He came to beat you!'"

BACKGROUND

Jackie Robinson was the first African American to play modern major league baseball. From 1947–1956 Robinson batted .311 in 1,382 games. In 1962, he was elected to the Baseball Hall of Fame, the first African American player so honored.

➤ In "Hero on the Ball Field," by Robert Peterson, students are introduced to a biography that slants positively toward its main character through the use of selected facts and clearly expressed opinions. Peterson's biography is written in third-person point of view, and his individual perspective is clearly one of strong appreciation for this baseball great.

➤ Students need to be able to point out phrases and words that show the author's opinion of Robinson (acrobatic fielder, best baserunner of his time, daring, hero in black communities, a leader) and distinguish these from facts that could be documented in other sources (signed with the Brooklyn Dodgers, stole 29 bases in 1947, retired in 1957, Hall of Fame election in 1962).

FOR DISCUSSION AND REFLECTION

➤ Why did Branch Rickey tell Robinson to curb his temper if he were abused or taunted by white players or fans? (Robinson represented all African Americans as he broke into the major leagues. Although he certainly might have felt angry or frustrated, by staying calm in the midst of taunts and threats, Robinson would not give his critics any "ammunition.")

➤ From what evidence can you infer that Robinson was a hero both on the field and off? (Students may point to the statistics indicating his baseball success, the honors received, and his role as a leader and spokesman for African Americans).

Writing

QUICK ASSESS

Do students' charts:

✓ cover a range of incidents?

✓ include thoughtful inferences about Robinson?

As students reread the biographical excerpt to complete the chart, advise them to identify specific incidents and infer what characteristics each incident shows about Robinson. For example, the fact that Robinson often stole bases showed his ability to play the game and his willingness to take a risk.

READING AND WRITING EXTENSIONS

➤ Invite students to bring in a sports article from a local newspaper or magazine. Have them discuss whether more fact or more opinion occurred in the article.

➤ Have students research the experiences of some of the other early African American major league stars, including Willie Mays, Hank Aaron, or Ernie Banks.

See also Answer Key, page 114

TWOIn His Own Words

Critical Reading

FOCUS
It is difficult for the writer of an autobiography to be objective about the events being described.

BACKGROUND
Robinson's autobiography, *I Never Had It Made*, offers a personal and less benign account of his breakthrough into baseball. While reading the excerpt, students focus on autobiography and first-person narrative. While this genre is limited because we know only the narrator's feelings, it is highly personal; we are inside the mind of the narrator. In the sample, Robinson reports the beginning of his friendship with Pee Wee Reese, a successful Dodger shortstop.

➤ Help students understand that Robinson concentrates on one personal incident when a teammate showed personal courage and open tolerance. No one could know Robinson's feelings but the man himself; players "sat in the dugout and pointed bats at me . . . . It was an incredibly childish display of bad will."

FOR DISCUSSION AND REFLECTION
➤ What can you infer from Robinson's reservation about meeting Reese: " I was aware that there might well be a real reluctance on Reese's part to accept me as a teammate"? (Reese was from Kentucky where there might still be much segregation of blacks. Also, Robinson might take over Reese's baseball position, so there could be professional jealousy.)

➤ How did the long and lasting friendship between Reese and Robinson begin? (It began at the time that Reese placed his arm around Robinson and faced a jeering crowd by saying, "Yell. Heckle. Do anything you want. We came here to play baseball.")

➤ What might have been going through Reese's mind at the time? (Responses may include nervousness, compassion, fear of the reaction of his teammates, respect for a fellow player.)

Writing

QUICK ASSESS
Do students' diagrams:
✔ list major similarities and differences?
✔ use specific details from the text?

Students complete a Venn diagram to compare the autobiography with the student news article. Remind students to place common elements in the middle and differences on the outside of the ellipses.

READING AND WRITING EXTENSIONS
➤ Ask students to read the full autobiography of Jackie Robinson or that of another minority person. Report orally on the opinions expressed by the narrator.

➤ Invite students to find a newspaper or magazine editorial in which the author has expressed some bias. Discuss together some of the examples they bring in.

Three Another Perspective

Critical Reading

FOCUS

Memoirs present readers with special insight that biographies cannot.

BACKGROUND

In "Another Perspective," students read from Sharon Robinson's memoir *Stealing Home*, in which bias is demonstrated through a daughter's point of view, the perspective of a child's remembrance of her father. The excerpt focuses on a 1957 incident in which nine black teenagers from Little Rock, Arkansas, began the court-ordered integration of schools. Arkansas Governor Orvall Faubus called out the Arkansas National Guard to prevent the integration at the all-white Little Rock Central High School. President Dwight D. Eisenhower sent federal troops to enforce the law, and the black students were admitted to Central.

➤ While Sharon Robinson's own childhood has been comfortable, she learns this is not true for all African Americans and begins to understand the influence her father had on attitudes toward black Americans: "I am sure that he also felt good playing a role, and grateful that the school experiences of his own children did not include such extreme displays of hatred."

FOR DISCUSSION AND REFLECTION

➤ Explain how Sharon's observations of her father on this occasion give readers more insight into Jackie Robinson. (Answers may be that he was generally a quiet man but worked up on this occasion, that the sound of his voice indicated they were discussing something serious, or that tears were building in his eyes.)

➤ Why did Minnie say she was following in Jackie's footsteps? (Just like Robinson broke in the segregated world of baseball, so too these high school students were entering an all-white high school in Arkansas.)

➤ Did Sharon understand her father's lesson on prejudice? (Yes, she dreamed of joining with Minnie and the others, forming "an impenetrable barrier" and conveying "an unstoppable message.")

Writing

QUICK ASSESS

Do students' lists:

✓ include examples from all three selections?

✓ give a range of Robinson's characteristics?

Students will brainstorm a list of characteristics that describe Jackie Robinson from all three selections (biography, autobiography, daughter's memoir).

READING AND WRITING EXTENSIONS

➤ Linda Rief, in *Seeking Diversity*, offers an exercise in which students map across a timeline of the five best and five worst events of their lives. Suggest that they begin by writing a long list and narrowing down to one incident. Ask students to write one scene of their lives from two points of view. For example, they could describe a birthday party from the point of view of a friend who attended and that of a grandparent at the party.

➤ Invite students to read from biographies, autobiographies, or memoirs by or about other sports heroes.

See also Answer Key, page 115

Four A Poetic Portrait

Critical Reading

FOCUS

Lucille Clifton writes in the language of compressed images:

Jackie Robinson "ran against walls / without breaking"

BACKGROUND

Lucille Clifton's poem "Jackie Robinson" offers a fourth perspective on the man. Less subjective than his own words and not biased from his devoted daughter's point of view, the poem still honors the man with selected, tight images.

➤ Review with students the difference between the way poetry and prose looks on a page. Point out that poetry uses line breaks, white space, and stanzas to organize and convey its meaning. For example, Clifton breaks a line after "walls" to emphasize that the walls could be literal or figurative. You may want to talk about the use of compressed language to create images and express feelings.

➤ Demonstrate with students the literal (dictionary) and figurative meanings of the words used in the poem—for example, walls could be barriers made of stone and barriers made by prejudice.

FOR DISCUSSION AND REFLECTION

➤ What is the meaning of the "whitestone fences"? (Students will probably say breaking into baseball, taunts to his family and Robinson from whites, the walls of a ballpark.)

➤ How can a man be "brave as a hit"? (A hit is a success in baseball. Robinson was brave as a first in his occupation. He was brave as a representative of all African Americans. Also, a hit ball challenges the players on the field.)

Writing

QUICK ASSESS

Do students' poems:

✓ use figurative meanings of words?

✓ model Clifton's style?

✓ show what makes the person special?

To help students brainstorm subjects for their poems, on the board create a list of different people they admire: friends, relatives, teachers, coaches, and so on. Begin by doing one poem collectively. After choosing one person, brainstorm again a list of words, phrases, titles, and actions associated with the person. Model how to rearrange words to form line breaks and images.

READING AND WRITING EXTENSIONS

➤ Have students find a sports article about a game that features a particular player. Ask them to create a "found poem" by rearranging the existing text into poetic form with line breaks and white space.

➤ Encourage students to read more poetry about baseball, especially "Teammates," by Peter Golenbock, in *Extra Innings* (edited by Lee Bennett Hopkins). It gives a poetic account of the autobiographical excerpt in which Pee Wee Reese put his arm around Robinson. Have students point out the images used by the poet and contrast them with Robinson's own words.

See also Answer Key, page 115

Five Thinking About Genres

Critical Reading

BACKGROUND

This lesson focuses on the four genres of biography, autobiography, personal accounts, and poetry and is designed to help students determine the strengths and weaknesses of each.

➤ Point out that a strength of biography is an objective stance by the author using factual details. A weakness is that the opinions expressed by the author are limited to his or her viewpoint.

➤ Review that a strength of autobiography and personal accounts is that they clearly express the opinion of the subject by giving access to information no one else would know. A weakness is that many facts are not utilized or are blurred by the bias of the person writing.

➤ Help students to see that strengths of poetry include strong use of imagery; tight, compressed language; and inferred opinions. The emotional power of poetry is evident while the short length often means lack of detail.

FOR DISCUSSION AND REFLECTION

➤ Which selection about Robinson did you enjoy the most? (Responses will vary, but push students to explain their reasoning.)

➤ Do you think it would be easy to write your autobiography? (Responses will vary.)

➤ Which selection do you think revealed the most interesting dimensions of Jackie Robinson's personality? (Responses will vary.)

Writing

QUICK ASSESS

Do students' collages:

✓ combine pictures and words?

✓ draw from all of the genres?

Encourage students to be creative as they create a collage, with words and pictures, that expresses the many sides of Jackie Robinson.

READING AND WRITING EXTENSIONS

➤ Work with the librarian to find other examples of poems written about famous people. Have students read the poems and discuss what bias may be evident.

➤ Invite students to write the first paragraph of the autobiography that they will write fifty years from now.

See also Answer Key, page 115

Unit Overview

In this unit, students explore the "art" of language by focusing on sensory images, metaphor, simile, and symbol. Through reading and responding to a variety of poetry, students will unlock the writing techniques essential to the poet's craft.

Literature Focus

Lesson	Literature
1. Show, Don't Tell	**Nikki Giovanni,** "knoxville, tennessee" (Poetry)
2. Conveying Feelings	**Pat Mora,** "Graduation Morning" (Poetry)
3. Making Comparisons	**Langston Hughes,** "Mother to Son" (Poetry)
4. Another Way to Compare	**Jane Yolen,** "Birthday Box" (Short Story)
5. Symbols	

Reading Focus

1. When you read works with sensory images, immerse yourself in the images to get a better understanding of the work and its meaning.
2. Writers use imagery in their writing to evoke specific feelings in readers about the subjects and ideas of their works.
3. When you read a metaphor, decide what qualities of an object, person, or idea the writer is trying to reveal through the comparison.
4. Writers use similes to give readers fresh insight into the qualities of objects, people, and ideas.
5. Writers use symbols to reveal qualities about objects, people, or ideas.

Writing Focus

1. Use sensory imagery to write a poem about a favorite season.
2. Create a collage about a particular emotion.
3. Write a poem based on a common metaphor.
4. Write a character sketch of a family member or friend, using original similes to reveal what makes the person special to you.
5. Draw a picture of an object that symbolizes you.

One Show, Don't Tell

Critical Reading

FOCUS

Poets use sensory imagery to give a "you are there" feeling to readers.

BACKGROUND

Nikki Giovanni is a talented African American poet and essayist. She was born in 1943, in Knoxville, the setting of this poem about family and personal relationships.

➤ This lesson presents sensory imagery as part of the art of writing. While students are familiar with the five senses, they often don't notice the details of how sensory imagery is used. For example, "I see" is not the sensory image. It is what is seen: "okra / and greens / and cabbage / and lots of / barbecue." It is not "I feel," but what is expressed as a sense of touch: "and go barefooted / and be warm / all the time . . . ."

FOR DISCUSSION AND REFLECTION

➤ What type of setting does Giovanni describe in her poem? (It is a country setting of summer, garden, church picnics, and mountains.)

➤ What relationships are included in the poem? (They are daughter with father and granddaughter with grandmother.)

➤ What do you notice about the form of the poem? (Students may point out that there is little punctuation, that it looks like a list, that there is much white space, and so on.)

➤ Does the poem remind you of any of your own summer memories? (Responses will vary.)

Writing

QUICK ASSESS

Do students' poems:

✓ use sensory imagery?

✓ focus on a season?

✓ use Giovanni's poem as a model?

As an introduction to writing a poem about a favorite season, ask students to bring in magazine pictures and photographs of scenes or vacation spots. Set up four centers in the room for summer, winter, autumn, and spring. Have students visit each center and freewrite a list of images for each season.

READING AND WRITING EXTENSIONS

➤ Have students create word banks like the magnetic poetry games. Advise them to include sensory words, color words, and specific nouns. Then have several students pool words and use as many as possible to create a free verse poem.

➤ Ask students to find out more information about the life and writing of Nikki Giovanni and have them present the information orally to the class.

See also Answer Key, page 115

Two Conveying Feelings

Critical Reading

FOCUS
Sensory images evoke strong feelings:

"Tears slide down her wrinkled cheeks. / Her eyes, *luceros*, stroke his face."

BACKGROUND

Pat Mora, an Hispanic poet, often writes about her culture. The Spanish-speaking settings she likes to use—a very different environment from Knoxville—evoke powerful emotions for the reader. The relationship between Lucero and the old Mexican housecleaner is presented with specific nouns (milk candy, creosote, scarf), adjectives (stubborn, cactus, small), and verbs (snared, running, pulled, hiding).

➤ Help students respond to the poem by jotting down their personal feelings to particular lines. By suggesting mood words—like happiness, sadness, anger, fear, gratitude, and pride—before reading the poem, students will better appreciate the effect of Mora's imagery.

FOR DISCUSSION AND REFLECTION

➤ What does the poet mean by the line: "Her eyes, *luceros*, stroke his face"? (The old woman's eyes reflected Lucero, were filled with his image of his graduation day, were filled with pride for him.)

➤ What are examples of unusual word choice in Mora's poem? (Responses may include "snared him with sweet coffee . . . ," "pulled stubborn cactus thorns / from his small hands . . . .")

➤ What contrast does Mora provide with the image of the "sparkling clothes"? (Answers include the formality of the occasion, the severity of the housecleaner's clothes, the strong black-and-white contrast, and so on.)

Writing

QUICK ASSESS
Do students' collages:

✓ display a particular emotion?

✓ creatively use images to convey mood?

Before students begin their collages, post several photographs on the board that depict a certain mood. Have students write a caption for the photographs. Then have them search through the magazines to create their own picture collage to demonstrate a particular mood. When they have their collage finished, suggest that they ask a peer to describe the mood that is depicted.

READING AND WRITING EXTENSIONS

➤ Bring in a copy of Chris Van Allsburg's picture book *The Mysteries of Harris Burdick*. Read aloud the preface which states that the book is a set of pictures with captions for short stories, but all of the stories were lost. Have students select one of the pictures and write a short story for the picture.

➤ Invite students to read Pat Mora's poem "Elena," which deals with the pain that occurs in a family when language becomes a barrier.

Three Making Comparisons

Critical Reading

FOCUS

In "Mother to Son," Hughes uses a striking metaphor:

"Well, son, I'll tell you: / Life for me ain't been no crystal stair."

BACKGROUND

In this lesson, students explore metaphor as one of the poet's arts. A metaphor makes a comparison between two unlike things without using *like* or *as* in the statement. However, for it to work, there needs to be some logic for the comparison, or the reader will not understand the connection between the images. When the poet carries the metaphor throughout the poem, it is called an extended metaphor. In "Mother to Son," the speaker is a mother who directly addresses her son and compares her life to a worn, broken staircase.

➤ Langston Hughes was a member of the Harlem Renaissance, a group of black writers in New York City during the 1920s and 1930s who protested against the social injustices toward African Americans. In particular, Hughes's poetry was revolutionary because it rebelled against classical form and often resembled the rhythm of speech or jazz: "I'se been a-climbin' on, / And reachin' landin's, / And turnin' corners . . . ."

FOR DISCUSSION AND REFLECTION

➤ Was the mother's life an easy one? (No, she describes problems in the images of tacks, splinters, torn-up boards, no carpet, and bare floor.)

➤ Does the mother encourage her son? (Yes, she tells how she kept "a-climbin' on, / And reachin' landin's / And turnin' corners," and she advises "Don't you set down on the steps / 'Cause you finds it kinder hard.")

Writing

QUICK ASSESS

Do students' poems:

✓ include a logical comparison?

✓ use images that support the extended metaphor?

With the Langston Hughes poem as a model, students will develop a poem about their own lives using an extended metaphor. On the board, list some suggestions that might work. Under each sample, brainstorm together images that could be part of the metaphor. (For the idea that life has not been a home run, for example, students might think of home runs, times at bat, strike-outs, hits, running to bases, sliding to home, boos from the crowd, and so on.)

READING AND WRITING EXTENSIONS

➤ Have students compile a class poetry anthology with the different poems completed and encourage them to illustrate their metaphors.

➤ Encourage students to select poetry more broadly by having each one choose a topic of interest. In the school library, help them find, read, and copy two poems about the topic. Ask them to write about the imagery, emotion, and figurative language used by the different poets.

Four Another Way to Compare

Critical Reading

FOCUS

Similes can help readers gain insight into characters:

"'It's empty,' I said, 'Is this a joke?' I turned to ask Mama, but she was gone. I mean, her body was there, but she wasn't. It was as if she was as empty as the box."

BACKGROUND

Jane Yolen has said about her own writing, "I don't care whether the story is real or fantastical, I tell the story that needs to be told." "The Birthday Box" is a strong, emotional story of a young daughter coping with her mother's death after a long battle with cancer. Award-winning Jane Yolen is a prolific writer of more than 170 books for children and young adults. All of her stories and poems are somehow rooted in her sense of family and self.

➤ Lesson Four focuses on simile as the writer's technique. Remind students that a simile creates a comparison between two unlike things using *like* or *as*. In this story, Jane Yolen uses similes to make her descriptions more precise and vivid: "needles . . . like teeth," "stars . . . like a map of the night sky," "skin like that old paper," "eyes . . . like the fall sky," and so on.

FOR DISCUSSION AND REFLECTION

➤ Why do you think Katie did not understand her mother's present? (It was beautifully wrapped but empty, and most young children would be surprised by that. She thought that "It's you" meant "it is for you." Because her mother died just as she received it, Katie had no time to talk about the present, and the box was put aside in her move.)

➤ What helped Katie to realize the importance of the birthday box? (After she remembered that her mother was a poet who carefully chose her words, Katie began to see how the box was like herself: empty but needing to be filled with words and memories.)

Writing

QUICK ASSESS

Do students' character sketches:

✓ use original similes?

✓ reveal personality?

As a prewriting activity before the students compose their character sketches, invite them to list important people in their lives. Have them write *ME* in a circle in the center of a page. In the next concentric circle, list the names of the people who live in their home; in the next circle, list the names of their other family members; in the next, list friends from school, neighborhood, teams, camps, and so on.

READING AND WRITING EXTENSIONS

➤ Read aloud the picture book *Owl Moon* by Jane Yolen. This story recounts a pleasant memory between a father and daughter as they walk out to the woods at night to hear the whooing of an owl. Invite students to write their own picture books about personal memories of times with a relative.

➤ Have students use construction paper, photos, drawings, advertisements, or pictures to illustrate one of the similes in their character sketches. Display these around the classroom.

Five Symbols

Critical Reading

FOCUS

Recognizing symbolic meaning can deepen our understanding of a story:

" 'It's you,' I whispered to the box. And then suddenly I knew. Mama had meant / was the box, solid and sturdy, maybe even beautiful or at least interesting on the outside. But I had to fill ....me up as well."

BACKGROUND

This lesson returns to the Jane Yolen story to explore the use of a symbol. You might begin the lesson by bringing in pictures that are symbols in our culture: the flag, the Statue of Liberty, the rose, or a gold medal. In small groups, have students discuss the significance of these familiar symbols. Help students recognize how labels, logos, and ad campaigns rely on the easy recognition of symbols and the public's associations with them.

➤ Spend some time discussing the story's title. Have students look at the beauty of the outside of the box and contrast it with the emptiness inside. Encourage them to think about how a box could symbolize a young girl.

FOR DISCUSSION AND REFLECTION

➤ What do you know of Katie's interests? (Answers may vary, but there are several clues that she enjoys writing. The presents include a pen, writing supplies, and a diary, and Katie turns to writing at the end.)

➤ When does Katie understand the symbolism of the box? (She understands on this first birthday without her mother, when she remembers her mother was a teacher and a poet and used words carefully.)

➤ Why does Yolen describe the box as beautiful, with "a pattern of cloud-filled skies"? (Responses will vary, but students may comment on Katie's later recognition that she herself was "maybe even beautiful or at least interesting on the outside.")

Writing

QUICK ASSESS

Do students' pictures:

✓ show neatness and creativity?

✓ have a caption explaining the symbol and its personal connection?

Students are asked to create a picture of an object that symbolizes themselves. Suggest some images—a soccer ball, a favorite collection, a vacation souvenir, something they made, and so on. After illustrating the symbol, students write a caption connecting the symbol to their lives.

READING AND WRITING EXTENSIONS

➤ Bring in books of poetry for students to read in small literature circles. Have them find, present, and explain symbols found in the poems.

➤ Focus on the advertisements of famous-name products. Have students discuss the meaning of the logos that companies choose for their products. (The Nike swish, for example, might suggest speed and athleticism.)

See also Answer Key, page 116

Unit Overview

Persuasive writing contains specific elements just as fiction and poetry do, and "The Art of Argument" is designed to help students better analyze persuasive writing and appreciate the significance of the thesis. Students learn how to support a thesis with facts, anecdotes, and examples, how to refute opposing arguments, and how and why they should understand the needs of the audience.

Literature Focus

	Lesson	Literature
1.	Thinking About Thesis	**Richard Carlson,** from *Don't Sweat the Small Stuff* (Nonfiction)
2.	Supporting Your Thesis	
3.	Using Facts and Statistics	**Louis L'Amour,** from "The Eternal Frontier" (Nonfiction–Science)
4.	Refute Opposition	**Sojourner Truth,** "Ain't I a Woman?" (Nonfiction–Social Studies)
5.	Understanding Audience	

Reading Focus

1. To be effective, an argument's thesis statement should be clear and memorable.
2. One way of supporting an argument is with anecdotes and examples.
3. When you read an argument, look for facts and figures that support the author's perspective.
4. By refuting the opposition, you can give additional strength to your side of the argument.
5. Understanding the needs of your audience can help you build a strong, persuasive argument.

Writing Focus

1. Maintain a record of actions connected to a thesis.
2. Compose anecdotal support for an argument.
3. List possible sources for supporting an argument.
4. Complete a chart on refuting opposing arguments.
5. Plan a persuasive argument.

One Thinking About Thesis

Critical Reading

FOCUS

At the center of Richard Carlson's essay is his thesis:

"Practicing random kindness is an effective way to get in touch with the joy of giving without expecting anything in return."

BACKGROUND

"Thinking About Thesis" introduces students to persuasive or argumentative essays. After choosing a topic for writing, an author needs to present a viewpoint or state an opinion on the topic, usually expressed in a thesis statement. In "Practice Random Acts of Kindness," Richard Carlson suggests "Practicing random kindness is an effective way to get in touch with the joy of giving without expecting anything in return." Be sure students recognize that the author wants to persuade his readers to believe this idea.

➤ Explain to students that Dr. Richard Carlson is a best-selling author of self-help guides and a consultant on how to reduce and control stress. His philosophy teaches a new way of relating to life, by calming down and living a less hectic and more meaningful, loving life. A family man who lives in northern California, Carlson urges small daily changes and uses examples of improvement from his own life to show how the advice works.

FOR DISCUSSION AND REFLECTION

➤ What are some of the random acts of kindness that Carlson presents to support his thesis? (Some responses include paying the tolls for others, picking up neighborhood litter, contributing to charity, and sending cash in an unmarked envelope.)

➤ Describe these random acts and their effects. (They are anonymous, spontaneous, from the heart; the recipient is not necessarily someone known to the giver. The reward is that the giver feels joy and maybe sets off a series of kind acts.)

Writing

QUICK ASSESS

Do students' logs:

✔ list a series of kind acts suggested by Carlson?

✔ express a personal response to doing the act of kindness?

Prepare students to test Carlson's thesis by placing them in small groups to brainstorm "potential" small acts of kindness that could occur at school and at home. Examples might be loaning someone lunch money, letting someone step ahead of you in line, calling a relative to say hello, picking up litter in school halls, and so on. Designate a particular day when each student will try to practice Carlson's acts of kindness.

READING AND WRITING EXTENSIONS

➤ Invite students to read essays from *Chicken Soup for the Teenage Soul*. Have them share the topics, theses, and arguments from selections of this book and then write their own essays.

➤ Have students write a petition for an improvement within the school. This might include a better lunch menu, no homework over long vacations, more money for music programs, and so on. Ask students to include the reasons for the change in their petitions.

See also Answer Key, page 116

Two Supporting Your Thesis

Critical Reading

FOCUS

Anecdotal support can add to the persuasiveness of an argument.

BACKGROUND

This lesson explains how to use anecdotal stories and examples to support an argument. Remind students that an anecdote is a short narrative that offers detail through a real story. Carlson's anecdote of drivers paying tolls for the cars following them on the San Francisco Bay Bridge area gives an example that is easily done, random, inexpensive, and real. Other examples of random kindness include picking up litter in the neighborhood, contributing to a charity, sending some cash in an unmarked envelope, saving an animal, and so on.

➤ Help students to see that many popular television programs revolve around personal stories and anecdotes—for example, *Unsolved Mysteries*, *People's Court*, and *Oprah*. By giving actual examples that can be documented, an essayist's argument becomes more legitimate.

FOR DISCUSSION AND REFLECTION

➤ Do you agree that receiving a random gift of kindness would create a chain reaction of kind acts? (Answers will vary, but urge students to support their opinions with their own anecdotal evidence.)

➤ What do you think of the kind act that Carlson develops in detail? (Responses will vary, but students should recognize that Carson concentrates on how drivers in the San Francisco Bay area paid the tolls for other drivers.)

➤ Have you ever performed "a random act of kindness"?

Writing

QUICK ASSESS

Do students' writings:

✔ present a clear opinion on a specific issue?

✔ develop anecdotal support for the thesis?

After brainstorming possible topics for a persuasive piece, students need to choose one topic and write three anecdotes to support their theses. The anecdotes should be concise and relevant to the topic.

READING AND WRITING EXTENSIONS

➤ Invite students to bring in editorials from a newspaper or magazine. In small groups, have them decide whether or not the argument presented is persuasive.

➤ Ask students to return to Latoya Hunter's diary in the "Essentials of Reading" unit. Based on her description of Freshman Day, have them write a letter for her school newspaper encouraging the end of the practice.

Three Using Facts and Statistics

Critical Reading

FOCUS

L'Amour uses specific facts and statistics to develop his argument.

BACKGROUND

Louis Dearborn L'Amour (1908–88) was an American author, most famous for his best-selling western novels, including *Hopalong Cassidy* (his first novel) and *Hondo*, his most popular. Many of his novels were turned into successful movies and television miniseries.

➤ Lesson Three presents an excerpt from L'Amour's essay, "The Eternal Frontier," which argues that the final frontier for man's exploration is outer space, beyond our solar system. The support L'Amour gives for the argument is figures and statistics rather than anecdotal stories. (Facts include that in 1900, there were 144 miles of surfaced roads; now there are more than 3,000,000. In the past seventy years we have developed the automobile, radio, television, transcontinental and transoceanic flight, the electrification of the country, and so on.)

FOR DISCUSSION AND REFLECTION

➤ Why do facts and statistics provide persuasive support? (Answers will vary.)

➤ How does L'Amour anticipate the argument that there is so much to do on earth that we shouldn't explore beyond it? (Student responses will vary. Elsewhere, L'Amour explained the human desire to explore the frontier by asserting, "If that [caution] had been the spirit of man we would still be hunters and food gatherers, growling over the bones of carrion in a cave somewhere. It is our destiny to move out, to accept the challenge, to dare the unknown.")

➤ Do you agree with L'Amour's argument? (Responses will vary.)

Writing

QUICK ASSESS

Do students' lists:

✔ identify a variety of sources?

✔ explain the type of information each source contains?

Students are asked to support the argument that computers or the Internet are the final frontiers. Have students work in pairs to create a working bibliography of sources that would contain information to support this topic.

READING AND WRITING EXTENSIONS

➤ Invite students to read one of L'Amour's western novels in the Sackett series—*To the Far Blue Mountains*, *The Lonely Man*, or *The Man from the Broken Hills*. Have them explain how the theme of adventure and exploration is developed.

➤ Encourage students to visit the NASA Web site at www.nasa.gov to research facts on current United States space explorations and share the information with the class.

Four Refute Opposition

Critical Reading

FOCUS

Refuting the opposition helps make an argument persuasive:

"That man over there says that women need to be helped into carriages, and lifted over ditches, and to have the best place everywhere. Nobody ever helps me into carriages … And ain't I a woman?"

BACKGROUND

"Refute Opposition" suggests that a persuasive argument is made stronger by anticipating the opposing or counter ideas to it and refuting these arguments when possible. By dealing with the objections to an idea, an argument can only be strengthened.

➤ Sojourner Truth (1797–1883) was an American abolitionist and advocate for women's rights. She was born into slavery but freed when the state of New York emancipated the slaves in 1828. A mystic, she took the name Sojourner Truth and began preaching on the issues of anti-slavery and women's rights. At one point, she advocated a "Negro State" in the West. An illiterate all of her life, Truth was an effective speaker who was even received by President Lincoln in the White House in 1864. Her famous speech at the Woman's Rights Convention of 1851 was directed at the words of a clergyman who had warned "if women continued their efforts to obtain 'rights,' they would lose the consideration and deference with which men treated them." The basis of her argument was to tell all that she had done and refute any opposition with the refrain of "Ain't I a Woman?"

FOR DISCUSSION AND REFLECTION

➤ What colorful language or use of vernacular makes Sojourner's speech so accessible to the audience? (Answers may include "something out of kilter," "white men will be in a fix pretty soon," "That's it, honey," "and now old Sojourner ain't got nothing more to say.")

➤ What are the topics that she addresses in this speech? (Students should identify the rights of blacks and women: "the Negroes of the South and the women at the North, all talking about rights . . . .")

Writing

QUICK ASSESS

Do students' responses:

✓ list three opposing arguments?

✓ explain how to refute each?

Students may want to work in groups as they choose argumentation topics and identify and refute potential opposing arguments.

READING AND WRITING EXTENSIONS

➤ Invite students to read an example of a famous persuasive speech such as Lincoln's "Gettysburg Address" or Martin Luther King, Jr.'s "I Have a Dream." In small groups, have them discuss the arguments presented in these great orations and explain what opposing arguments might be.

➤ Encourage students to research some of the other proponents of abolition and women's rights, perhaps John Brown, Susan B. Anthony, Lucretia Mott, or Elizabeth Cady Stanton. Have them summarize the arguments that these advocates made in their speeches.

See also Answer Key, page 116

Five Understanding Audience

Critical Reading

FOCUS

Opinions on a topic are expressed differently depending on the anticipated audience.

BACKGROUND

This lesson helps students understand the importance of knowing one's audience when presenting an argument. *Audience* refers to the readers and listeners for a speech or reading. Help students understand that the language that a writer selects should connect to the audience and anticipate who they are, what they may already know or think they know about the subject, and what their feelings about the topic are likely to be.

➤ The language of Sojourner Truth is familiar and homey as she uses words like "children" and "honey" to show a personal connection to her listeners. However, with this casual speech, she tries to convince women to stand up for their rights. L'Amour is writing to his readers or fans who know he is preoccupied with the western frontier: "The question I am most often asked is, 'Where is the frontier now?'" L'Amour expects that his audience will agree that space is the next frontier. Carlson seems to be directing his persuasive speech to adults who drive and read bumper stickers. He tries to convince them of the value of performing acts of kindness.

FOR DISCUSSION AND REFLECTION

➤ How might the language of a speech change if it is written for an audience of adults or an audience of your peers? (Answers will vary but may include that language will be less formal with peers, may contain current references to slang or ideas not commonly known by adults, and so on.)

➤ What changes would L'Amour have to make to his speech to make it more current? (His statistics and details would have to be more recent—for example, referring to the space shuttle program, the use of the Internet, the use of satellites, and so on.)

Writing

QUICK ASSESS

Do students' plans:

✓ have a clear thesis and a variety of support?

✓ list several opposing arguments?

✓ analyze their intended audience?

Students plan a persuasive argument, incorporating a thesis, identifying supporting details, anticipating opposing arguments, and demonstrating their understanding of the audience.

READING AND WRITING EXTENSIONS

➤ Invite students to write a speech to argue that the hours of an upcoming school dance should be extended. First, have them write a speech to present to school officials and then revise it for an audience of parents.

➤ Invite students to find local essay contests that ask for persuasive writing: DARE programs, SADD programs, Rotary and Kiwanis programs, newspaper contests, and so forth. Encourage them to choose one contest to enter. Have students share the essays they write.

See also Answer Key, page 116

Unit Overview

In this unit, students will immerse themselves in the works of Yoshiko Uchida. Through reading and responding to excerpts from a novel, a folk tale, a memoir, and her autobiography, students will learn about her life, understand her interest in writing about Japanese Americans, and explore aspects of her craft.

Literature Focus

	Lesson	Literature
1.	A Writer's Heritage	from "The Princess of Light" (Folk Tale)
2.	A Writer's Identity	from *The Invisible Thread* (Autobiography)
3.	A Writer's Language	from *Journey Home* (Fiction)
4.	A Writer's Themes	from *Desert Exile* (Memoir)
5.	A Writer's Intent	

Reading Focus

1. Authors, like many people, explore questions like "Who am I?" and "Where do I belong?"
2. When you read an autobiography, watch for the ways the author answers the questions: "Who am I?" and "How do I fit in?" These questions will help you see how the author views himself or herself.
3. Writers use sensory language in order to give readers a "you are there" feeling.
4. Understanding an author's themes can help you connect your reading to your own life.
5. Some authors write with the intention of conveying to you, the reader, something they believe is important or meaningful.

Writing Focus

1. Write a letter from the perspective of Uchida.
2. Complete a diagram exploring the different aspects of Uchida's identity.
3. Categorize Uchida's use of sensory language.
4. Write a journal entry about one of Uchida's themes.
5. Use a graphic organizer to display notes from the unit.

One A Writer's Heritage

Critical Reading

FOCUS

Yoshiko Uchida on her Japanese heritage:

"Most important, however, my years in Japan had made me aware of a new dimension to myself as a Japanese American and deepened my respect and admiration for the culture that had made my parents what they were."

BACKGROUND

Yoshiko Uchida (1921–1992) was born in California. She lived there with her parents and sister peacefully for twenty years before World War II and the internment of many Japanese Americans in camps in California and Utah. While these camps were not the death camps used in Europe at the time, they were concentration camps where large groups of Japanese Americans were held for the final three years of the war. Through an executive order, President Franklin D. Roosevelt imprisoned 120,000 people in these camps. Yoshiko Uchida and her family were interned at the Topaz camp in Utah. During this time Uchida did much writing, often returning to the stories of her heritage to comfort her in times of crisis. She remembered that her mother would often read Japanese stories to her sister, Keiko, and her.

➤ Lesson One focuses on a re-telling of a folk tale by Uchida. Help students to see that they can learn much from the folk tale about the beliefs within the Japanese culture.

FOR DISCUSSION AND REFLECTION

➤ What important values seem central to the Japanese in this folk tale? (Answers may include hard work, importance of children, religion, and use of money for family.)

➤ What is the significance of the daughter being named "Princess of Light"? (Students may respond that she was golden in color like the gold coins and shining bamboo, that she was extremely beautiful and valuable to the old couple, that Uchida herself is a daughter, and so on.)

Writing

QUICK ASSESS

Do students' letters:

✓ use Uchida's point of view?

✓ answer the questions about identity?

After sharing the details about heritage and culture culled from the folk tale, students assume the identity of Yoshiko Uchida and write a letter home to her parents explaining what she has learned about herself through the re-acquaintance with Japanese folk tales.

READING AND WRITING EXTENSIONS

➤ Invite students to read Sheila Hamanaka's *The Journey*, a picture book based on her twenty-six-foot mural relating the history of the Japanese Americans in western United States.

➤ Encourage students to read more of Uchida's folk tales in her books, *The Dancing Kettle and Other Japanese Folk Tales*, *The Magic Listening Cap: More Folk Tales from Japan*, and *The Sea of Gold*. As a class, make a mural displaying some of the characters and images within the tales.

See also Answer Key, pages 116-117

TWO A Writer's Identity

Critical Reading

FOCUS

Yoshiko Uchida in *Something About the Author:*

"I lived in a society that in general made me feel different and not as good as my white peers .... All I longed for in those early years was to be like everyone else and to be viewed as an American."

BACKGROUND

Even before the tragedy of Japanese American internment, Yoshiko Uchida felt the separation from white America. In her autobiography, she shows that cultural understanding of Japanese Americans was not prevalent when she was a young girl. In both junior high and high school she felt "alienated and excluded" from the social activities of her white classmates. For example, she often was confined to Japanese students' clubs.

➤ "A Writer's Identity" focuses on Uchida's autobiography, *The Invisible Thread*, and asks students to reflect on her search for identity. The excerpt shows her ambivalence with her own identity, sometimes feeling Japanese like her parents, sometimes feeling American as she recites the Pledge of Allegiance in school, and sometimes feeling a blend of the two cultures.

FOR DISCUSSION AND REFLECTION

➤ How do we see that Uchida is self-conscious about her identity at a young age? (Among possible answers are that teachers could not pronounce her name correctly and that she longed for blond hair, blue eyes, and a simple name like Mary Anne Brown or Betty Johnson.)

➤ How does this selection reveal instances of racial prejudice? (Answers may include that Uchida was not allowed to swim in all public pools, and certain hairdressers did not cut Japanese hair.)

➤ Why does Uchida say that she loved her country "maybe even more" than other Americans? (Student answers will vary but may include that, because of her Japanese heritage, she did not take America or its culture for granted.)

Writing

QUICK ASSESS

Do students' diagrams:

✓ give evidence of all three segments of Uchida's identity?

✓ include the reactions of others to her?

Using their response notes from the selection, students should work in small groups to organize the details into three columns: those when she feels Japanese, those when she feels American, and those when she feels a blend of both cultures.

READING AND WRITING EXTENSIONS

➤ Invite students to read Hadley Irwin's novel, *Kim Kimi*, which describes an adopted girl's search for her heritage and compare that story to the one that Uchida tells.

➤ Have students write about a time when they felt they didn't fit in or when they wondered "Who am I?"

See also Answer Key, page 117

Three A Writer's Langauge

Critical Reading

FOCUS

Paying attention to a writer's choice of language can enrich our enjoyment of a work.

BACKGROUND

Yoshiko Uchida is a very prolific writer with more than thirty-one children's books, more than thirty-five short stories for anthologies, and several books for adults. Her writings include a variety of genres: folk tales, picture books, short stories, novels, non-fiction, and autobiography. Throughout, she often uses sensory language, or images appealing to the five senses.

➤ Lesson Three presents a selection from *Journey Home*, the sequel to *Journey to Topaz*, that describes the time when the Japanese Americans were released from the camps after the war. Students should have no trouble finding images connecting to sight, touch, smell, taste, and sound. Help them to think of the feelings associated with powerful description, such as "screaming desert wind," "eerie, unreal world," and "sting of sand and pebbles."

FOR DISCUSSION AND REFLECTION

➤ How does Uchida show the fear and pain of Yuki during the dust storm? (Responses will vary, but students may point to her striking description of the "great choking clouds of dust" that caused her to double over.)

➤ What conflicts are portrayed in this selection? (Responses should include man against nature, as Yuki struggles against the storm, and man against man, as she avoids the military's barbed wire.)

➤ How does Uchida's writing make you feel that "you are there"? (Responses will vary but will probably include some sensory images such as the "choking clouds of dust.")

Writing

QUICK ASSESS

Do students' webs:

✓ include a variety of sensory words?

✓ categorize the words accurately?

After collecting sensory images from the selection, students complete a web that categorizes Uchida's use of sensory language.

READING AND WRITING EXTENSIONS

➤ Suggest that students use the details from *Journey Home* to make an illustration that could accompany and complement the passage.

➤ Ask students to choose one of the photographs in their *Daybook* and write a poem that it inspires. Encourage them to use imagery that appeals to all of the senses.

See also Answer Key, page 117

Four A Writer's Themes

Critical Reading

FOCUS

Yoshiko Uchida on her childhood journal:

"I was trying to hold on to and somehow preserve the magic as well as the joy and sadness of certain moments in my life."

BACKGROUND

Lesson Four asks students to trace the two themes, or underlying messages, that reoccur in Uchida's writing: pride in one's ancestry and courage during times of trouble.

➤ Yoshiko Uchida's early writings are set in Japan with Japanese protagonists. Remind students that the Issei are the generation of Japanese born in Japan, while the Nisei are the first American-born Japanese. In the early seventies, Uchida focused on the atrocity of Japanese American internment. In the third phase of her work, she focused on Japanese Americans. She states in *Language Arts* magazine, " I saw the need to reinforce the self-knowledge and pride of young Japanese Americans . . . to give them a remembrance of their culture and their own particular history."

➤ Uchida was brought to the internment camp of Topaz after she graduated from college. While in Topaz she kept herself busy teaching second grade students while her sister organized nursery schools.

FOR DISCUSSION AND REFLECTION

➤ What were some of the hardships endured by the Issei? (Students should mention the enormous financial losses, personal indignities, and sacrifices for their children.)

➤ What dignity did the Issei exhibit in imprisonment? (They remained steadfast and strong in spirit, made homes of barracks, remained nurturing, encouraged education, and so on.)

➤ Ask students to think about whether anyone in their own families has endured hardships or made sacrifices for their children.

Writing

QUICK ASSESS

Do students' entries:

✔ focus on their heritage or courage?

✔ demonstrate a personal response to the theme?

After sharing the themes found in the excerpt of *Desert Exile*, students write a journal entry describing a time that showed courage or demonstrated pride in heritage. To prepare for this, invite students to list family traditions that they associate with their heritage. Display these on the board for all to see. For the alternative topic, help students see that courage is not always related to physical bravery.

READING AND WRITING EXTENSIONS

➤ Invite students to describe a moment when they saw someone acting courageously—someone they knew or a stranger.

➤ After reading aloud Uchida's picture book *The Bracelet*, have students make a picture book based on their reading of the autobiographical excerpt from *The Invisible Thread*.

Five A Writer's Intent

Critical Reading

FOCUS

Yoshiko Uchida on why she writes:

"I write to celebrate our common humanity, for I feel the basic elements of humanity are present in all of our strivings."

BACKGROUND

"A Writer's Intent" explores Yoshiko Uchida's own desire for her writing to dispel stereotypes, honor the first generation of Japanese through their culture, and find the connections between all members of humanity. Discuss with students some of the various reasons different writers might have for writing.

➤ Students are asked to reread and reflect upon the preceding lessons in the unit, finding details that show Uchida as a writer, a storyteller, and a teacher. You may find it helpful to share some of your own thoughts on what Yoshiko Uchida's writings have taught you.

FOR DISCUSSION AND REFLECTION

➤ What are some of the topics Uchida's writing emphasizes? (Among possible answers are the importance of children and religion to the Japanese family, the harshness of the internment camps, and the resilience of the Issei to their hardships.)

➤ How would you describe the elements of her writing? (Responses will vary but may include sensory images, references to her travel to Japan, historical facts, and so on.)

➤ Is it possible for writers both to entertain their readers and to teach them a lesson simultaneously? (Students' answers will vary, but you should encourage them to refer to specific writers and writings.)

Writing

QUICK ASSESS

Do students' graphic organizers:

✓ include information for all three categories?

✓ indicate understanding of the author's writings?

Help students to summarize in a graphic organizer what they have learned about Uchida as a writer, a storyteller, and a teacher. Students could work in groups to display this information in a tri-fold booklet that they could illustrate.

READING AND WRITING EXTENSIONS

➤ Invite students to write an editorial about the negative effects of stereotyping and prejudice within their school, town, or country. Encourage them to try to publish their piece in a school or local newspaper.

➤ Have the class work together to create a list of television shows or films that they believe negatively stereotype a group of people—for example, teenagers, senior citizens, stay-at-home moms, scientists, and so forth. Have them discuss the causes of such stereotyping.

See also Answer Key, page 117-118

Unit Overview

This unit focuses on the three levels of reader response: factual, interpretive, and evaluative. As students read Bailey White's short story "Turkeys," Shirley Jackson's "Charles," and Leo Tolstoy's fable "The King and the Shirt," they will improve their abilities to respond to literature in different ways and, as a result, discover how to increase their understanding and enjoyment.

Literature Focus

Lesson	Literature
1. Factual Response	**Bailey White**, "Turkeys" (Short Story)
2. Interpretive Response	**Shirley Jackson**, "Charles" (Short Story)
3. Supporting Your Views	**Shirley Jackson**, "Charles" (Short Story)
4. Evaluative Response	**Leo Tolstoy**, "The King and the Shirt" (Fable)
5. Connecting to Your Life	

Reading Focus

1. Asking factual questions such as who, what, when, where, and how can help you understand and connect with what you read.
2. To interpret a selection, begin by asking "why" questions about the characters.
3. A reader's interpretations need to be supported with evidence from the selection.
4. When you make an evaluative response, you form an opinion about what you have read.
5. Relating literature to your own life can add meaning to the selection and help you get the most out of your reading.

Writing Focus

1. Write the opening paragraphs for an article.
2. Write "why" questions and answers about characters in a story.
3. Fill out a character interpretation chart.
4. Evaluate a fable based on ratings of plot, characters, writing style, and the moral lesson.
5. Write a journal entry that explains a personal connection to one of the three selections.

One Factual Response

Critical Reading

FOCUS

Bailey White shares a memorable, fact-filled tale of measles and turkeys from the 1950s:

"One hundred percent pure wild turkey!"

BACKGROUND

Lesson One focuses on the factual level of writing and is designed to show students that they need to ask factual questions to understand important information, the things that "really" happen in the story. Even though Bailey White's story is a personal anecdote, students need to realize that it is filled with facts. One reason why people enjoy reading historical fiction, as their experience reading this piece might illustrate, is because the mixture of facts and story make learning so enjoyable.

➤ White has written a delightful piece that will bring a smile to the readers' faces as they unfold the tale of a young child with measles who helps incubate some wild turkey eggs into snuggling, fuzzy chicks. Students will enjoy the descriptive style of writing while searching for all of the factual clues in the piece. Most of the factual clues will be easy to locate, but it's important that when students are trying to locate the setting that they get beyond "in a house" and dig for more details, hinted at by the "Carolina parakeet," as a rural, piney woods area in the South.

FOR DISCUSSION AND REFLECTION

➤ Would you enjoy learning about wild turkeys as much if you had just read an impersonal encyclopedia article about them? (Answers will vary, but students will likely answer no. It's more fun and easier to hook on to material that is presented in a story format.)

➤ What items in the story can you find that aren't facts, but interpretations? (Answers may include "cruel jokes," "sensible child," "the world is a worse place," and "I like to think they [the turkeys] are all descendants . . . .")

Writing

QUICK ASSESS

Do students' openings:

✓ include adequate factual information?

✓ grab the readers' interest?

✓ include quotations?

Encourage students to review their response notes before they use their reporting skills to write a lead for their newspaper article on the Bailey White story. The story will need quotes as well as "voice" or "color" to make it interesting to the readers. Suggest that they try a bit of humor and possibly add a sketch or picture to enhance the writing.

READING AND WRITING EXTENSIONS

➤ Have the class write personal narratives about an interesting experience with an animal—at a zoo, in the wild, on a farm, in their neighborhood, at a park. Remind students to include some factual information.

➤ Let students choose an animal cracker from a box and write an original comic strip about the animal they select. Encourage them to title their creations and to use facts to support a six-section tale about their animal.

See also Answer Key, page 118

Two Interpretive Response

Critical Reading

FOCUS

Sometimes the reader has to untangle the mystery by interpreting the inferential clues scattered along the path to a surprise ending.

BACKGROUND

Often just reading for facts doesn't tell the "whole" story. Students need to realize that there are subtleties and nuances associated with characters' actions and thoughts that tell a lot about them and why they do what they do.

➤ Lesson Two helps students see that the "why" of the story is just as important as the facts of a story. Learning to read between the lines to fill in missing pieces or expand one's understanding of the meaning and the characters takes practice. This is a good time to help students learn to use details and examples from the text to support their ideas. Inferential judgments can be made from what characters do, say, and think, even from what others say and think about them. The most memorable stories are those that let the reader use his or her imagination to fill in the blanks. When an author tells us too much, the story becomes boring and predictable.

FOR DISCUSSION AND REFLECTION

➤ What can you infer about Laurie from the story? (His behavior has changed since starting kindergarten, and he has been influenced by Charles's behavior at school; he does naughty things; he laughs a lot and acts overconfident, as if he were covering up something.)

➤ How do his mom and dad feel about his behavior? (Mom takes it seriously by discussing it with her husband and repeatedly questioning Laurie. Dad doesn't seem too worried, dismissing things with a casual "boys will be boys" attitude.)

➤ What prediction can you make about the end of the story based on clues in the story thus far? (Answers will vary, but based on facts so far, students might think that Charles will end up in the principal's office or get in some kind of trouble with the teacher or at home.)

Writing

QUICK ASSESS

Do students' questions and answers:

✔ show an inferential understanding of the characters?

✔ use examples from the story as support?

As students think of other people that they have known who are similar to Charles and write questions to match with characters from the story, remind them that they will need examples from the story to support their "why" questions.

READING AND WRITING EXTENSIONS

➤ Invite students to illustrate the story with caricatures of Laurie, Charles, Mom, and Dad and share the pictures with their classmates.

➤ Have students work with a partner to create a storyboard of the story "Charles," using captions and illustrations.

Three Supporting Your Views

Critical Reading

FOCUS

Active readers think about why characters act the way they do.

BACKGROUND

Just as we learn to read a person's body language and tone of voice for clues about how they regard us, we can do the same thing with a piece of writing. If we are talking to someone who is sitting with their arms folded, looking out the window and yawning, we can assume that he or she isn't very interested in our conversation. Similarly, we can pick up clues in our reading that will be evidence or support for our assumptions about characters.

➤ It is a very difficult task for students to learn how to support their interpretations. Encourage them to get in the habit of using examples from the writing to defend their interpretations by saying, "I know this is true, because . . . ."

➤ For instance, Laurie seems to have changed from a sweet preschooler to a naughty, mischievous child: "I know this is true because he comes home and slams the door, yells in a raucous shout, uses bad grammar, is disrespectful to his parents, and finds bad behavior humorous. He's boastful and rude at the dinner table. His shrugs and laughter suggest his disregard of authority." Once students get into the habit of looking for evidence to support their ideas and interpretations, their writing will improve and show more depth.

FOR DISCUSSION AND REFLECTION

➤ Can you infer that Laurie's mom and his teacher were unsure of what to expect from each other at the PTA meeting? (Responses may vary, but students should note how they maneuvered up to one another cautiously and smiled.)

➤ Does Charles's behavior seem typical of young children starting kindergarten? (Answers will vary but may be based on personal experience. Probably students will think his behavior is challenging and out of line.)

➤ How do you know that there's been a change in Charles during the third and fourth week at school? (Laurie reports different behaviors, such as that he passed out crayons and picked up books.)

Writing

QUICK ASSESS

Do students' charts:

✓ give an accurate interpretation of each character?

✓ use several examples of support from the story?

Students give their opinion of Jackson's story and then write interpretations of each character in chart format. Make sure students understand that they can describe the characters any way they want as long as they find proof from the story as support.

READING AND WRITING EXTENSIONS

➤ Ask students to read Shirley Jackson's "The Lottery" and write about the clues she provides for the story's powerful ending.

➤ Have students write a children's story about their own kindergarten experiences, making sure that one of the criteria of the story is that it have strong characters supported with lots of behavioral details.

See also Answer Key, page 118

Four Evaluative Response

Critical Reading

FOCUS

To evaluate what you have read, ask yourself "What do I think about this selection?"

BACKGROUND

In Lesson Four, students will explore the process of making judgments about what they read. As you begin this lesson, help students to recognize that they are constantly evaluating, sorting out the good from the bad. Every day they voice their opinions about TV shows, movies, restaurants, friends, music, books, products, and so on. They might do an informal evaluation by thinking to themselves that a novel has merit and was well written and enjoyable, so much so that they pass the book along to a friend. On the other hand, they might compose a more formal evaluation as they complain to a head of a company about a product or a service that did or didn't meet their expectations.

➤ In this lesson, students explore how to make an evaluation of a fable by Leo Tolstoy. Tolstoy, perhaps Russia's greatest writer of realistic fiction, is most widely known for his novels, *War and Peace* and *Anna Karenina*. These magnificent novels reveal Tolstoy's desire for a quiet life in close harmony with nature as well as a belief in moral duty and a love of family.

FOR DISCUSSION AND REFLECTION

➤ Were you satisfied with the ending? (Answers will vary but may include that the end forces readers to think about the meaning of the story.)

➤ Why do you think the fable is so short? (One possible answer is that its brevity adds to its impact on the reader and makes one think of all the things that make us "unhappy.")

➤ Explain the line, "but the happy man was so poor that he had no shirt." (The moral is that if we remain happy and positive, nothing else matters; life is what you make it.)

Writing

QUICK ASSESS

Do students' recommendations:

✔ explain why or why not the fable is recommended?

✔ support their opinions with specifics?

Once the students rate the four aspects of the fable—plot, characters, writing style, and moral lesson—they'll write their recommendation to a friend based on their ratings. They could structure their writing with a paragraph about each topic of the ratings. The first paragraph could deal with the plot, the second paragraph would discuss the characters, and so on.

READING AND WRITING EXTENSIONS

➤ Have the class brainstorm a list of things that make them happy. See how many ideas they can assemble. Let students pick one to write about in the form of a fable, using Tolstoy's fable as a model.

➤ Invite students to create a class book of proverbs that they interpret and illustrate.

Five Connecting to Your Life

Critical Reading

FOCUS

Connecting on a personal level with a piece of literature is a powerful reading experience:

"When one cries, the other tastes salt."

BACKGROUND

Connections are what reading is all about. Lesson Five demonstrates for the students how a selection can remind them of certain experiences or memories that may be similar to what they have experienced. Of course, not every piece will connect to every reader, but depending on one's background and life experiences, there are usually ways to connect to almost every piece of writing in some way, after thoughtful reflection. This reflection forces students to stretch their imaginations and move beyond the printed word. Help students to see that the more they can connect with a main character, a setting, a plot or a theme, the more they can make the story their own.

FOR DISCUSSION AND REFLECTION

➤ Why is it important to make connections to literature? (Answers will vary, but they could include so that you relate to the main character's actions and feelings, so you can compare what you'd do in the same situation, or so you can relate your experiences to those of the main character.)

➤ Which of the three selections offers a viewpoint to which you can connect? (Answers will most likely be the story of Charles and his antics at school.)

➤ What are some other stories you've read in which you identified with the main character or the situation in the story? (Answers will vary, but you should urge students to cite specific reasons.)

➤ What kinds of writing do you find most difficult to connect to your life? (Answers will vary.)

Writing

QUICK ASSESS

Do students' journal entries:

✓ focus on one selection?

✓ show a personal connection?

By filling in a chart that lists the three selections from this unit, students will have the opportunity to connect with characters, setting, experiences, and the author's viewpoint. They will draw on this information to write a journal entry about the selection they connected to the most.

READING AND WRITING EXTENSIONS

➤ Have students work in small groups to transform their journal entries into reader's theater productions, assigning parts to different characters and writing dialogue for each character.

➤ Have students select a popular fairy tale with which they can make personal connections. Encourage them to write a paragraph about those connections.

Unit Overview

In "Reading Nonfiction: Factual Stories," students explore the world of ideas and facts as they read high-interest selections by Patricia Lauber, Charles Kuralt, and Maxine Kingston. Students will focus on understanding the main idea, analyzing causes and effects, drawing conclusions, and considering comparisons as they increase their understanding—and enjoyment— of nonfiction writing.

Literature Focus

	Lesson	Literature
1.	Big Picture, Small Parts	**Patricia Lauber,** from *Volcano* (Nonfiction–Science)
2.	Broad Statements	**Patricia Lauber,** from *Volcano* (Nonfiction–Science)
3.	Why and How	**Charles Kuralt,** from *On the Road with Charles Kuralt* (Nonfiction)
4.	If . . . Then . . .	
5.	Alike and Unlike	**Maxine Hong Kingston,** from "A Sea Worry" (Nonfiction)

Reading Focus

1. Sorting out main ideas and details can help you understand expository writing.
2. When you make generalizations based on your reading, you discover your own ways to apply the author's ideas.
3. Considering causes and effects helps you connect ideas as you read.
4. Drawing conclusions helps you think more deeply about the meaning of what you read.
5. Comparing and contrasting ideas helps you understand and analyze what you read.

Writing Focus

1. Identify the main idea and supporting details in a selection.
2. Write generalizations based on detailed information from a selection.
3. Complete a cause-and-effect chart.
4. Draw conclusions based on details from your reading.
5. Use a Venn diagram to compare and contrast ideas and draw conclusions.

One Big Picture, Small Parts

Critical Reading

FOCUS

Good writers supply lots of details to support their main points.

BACKGROUND

Lesson One introduces students to expository writing and the sorting out of main idea and supporting details. Patricia Lauber's *Volcano* is a nonfiction piece that plays out like an adventure film in the reader's head. It is often a minute-by-minute account of the events surrounding the eruption of Mount St. Helens. The details are descriptive, and students should enjoy reading this piece as they search for the main idea.

➤ Mount St. Helens was one of the most active volcanoes in the Cascade Mountains, 95 miles south of Seattle. Geologists predicted that she would erupt before the year 2000, and she did just that on the morning of May 18, 1980, at 8:32 a.m. Volcanic explosions blasted away more that 1,000 feet from the peak and created a huge crater. The eruption was the first to occur in the continental United States (outside Alaska) since 1917. The eruption resulted in 57 deaths, and destruction covered an area of some 230 miles.

➤ It may be helpful to have students think of Lauber's piece in terms of a concrete picture or shape, such as the concentric circles that a stone makes when thrown into a pond or the outer layer of an onion. The outermost layer or circle would be the biggest or main idea—what the piece is "really" about.

FOR DISCUSSION AND REFLECTION

➤ What is the scientific explanation for the volcanic eruption? (A volcano is an opening in the earth's surface through which lava, hot gases, and rock fragments burst forth, as melted rock from deep within the earth blasts through the surface.)

➤ What was the difference between the geologists' and the people's impression of the volcano? (People saw the mountain as a friendly, pleasant place to visit, while geologists viewed it as dangerous.)

➤ How do you think Patricia Lauber obtained all of her data? (Answers will vary but may include interviews, eyewitness accounts, newspapers, scientists, and others.)

Writing

QUICK ASSESS

Do students' idea wheels:

✔ identify the main idea?

✔ show supporting details?

Have students share interesting details in the selection and discuss any questions that remain about the volcano. You might suggest that they mark details found in the text in two distinct colors that support the "people" and the "scientists" parts of the main idea. Then they will record these details on their main idea wheel.

READING AND WRITING EXTENSIONS

➤ Invite students to do further research on other active volcanoes in the United States and share their findings with the class.

➤ Bring in pictures or videos of Mount St. Helens before and after the destruction to share with the class. Have students write a poem about an image that struck them.

See also Answer Key, page 119

Two Broad Statements

Critical Reading

FOCUS
One way to connect to nonfiction is to make your own generalizations.

BACKGROUND

Lesson Two helps students improve their abilities to make generalizations from their reading, using details to support their ideas. Point out that to keep generalizations accurate, students must not make them too broad. They need to avoid falling into the trap of "absolutes" by using such words as *all, always, none,* or *never.* Instead, make sure they use qualifiers such as *mostly, sometimes, usually, often,* and *seldom.*

➤ Students might need to practice this skill with oral discussion about subjects with which they are familiar. For example, instead of saying that the Chicago Bulls are always the best basketball team in the NBA, students should qualify the statement by saying that the Bulls have been the best team in the NBA in recent years, and that they have six recent championship rings to prove it! Kids love sports and will quickly see the correlation between supported generalizations and generalizations that are so broad that they can't be qualified.

FOR DISCUSSION AND REFLECTION

➤ What do you think is the most vivid detail in the selection? (Answers will vary, but they may include the hot steam rising from the blast, the "stone wind" that flattened forests, or the darkness resulting from the ash cloud.)

➤ What kind of warning do you think people received? (The warning was difficult, because they had trouble pinpointing the time of the eruption. Once it came, there was very little time to escape to safety.)

➤ Was there any good that came from this natural disaster? (Answers will vary, but students may focus on increased understanding of these natural phenomena, people working together to rebuild after the tragedy, and so forth.)

Writing

QUICK ASSESS
Do students' generalizations:

✔ show understanding of the selection?

✔ identify supporting details?

✔ use qualifiers?

After reviewing both selections for information about the scientists involved with this phenomenon, students try to make a generalization about the scientists' efforts, using specific details as support.

READING AND WRITING EXTENSIONS

➤ Put students into small groups and have each group record its different generalizations on a large piece of paper, making sure that each can be supported with details from the story. Then, have each group create and present a radio or TV news broadcast that would report what happened on May 18, 1980.

➤ Let students make sketches based on their visualization of a vivid scene from the selection for a "Volcano" bulletin board. They could also include research information about particular volcanoes, such as Mount St. Helens, Haleakala, Surtsey, and others.

See also Answer Key, page 119

Three Why and How

Critical Reading

FOCUS

From *On the Road with Charles Kuralt*:

"If you don't try to make the world just a little bit nicer when you leave here, what is the reason for man's existence in the first place?"

BACKGROUND

Lesson Three focuses the student on cause (the "why did it happen") and effect (the "how it affects us") in expository writing. Students will enjoy Charles Kuralt's tale about Mr. Misenheimer and his garden, yet probably wonder why anyone would do such a thing as he did. And then to think that Haeja Namkoong followed in his footsteps is even more surprising. The students will probably say they have difficulty thinking of anyone as caring and as sensitive as Mr. Misenheimer, but remind them that the person could be someone they know about but haven't met.

➤ Charles Kuralt, who joined CBS News in 1957, was one of the most distinguished voices in American journalism, as he delivered the news with a serene, reflective style that became his trademark. He was an author and reporter who cared about both the people he wrote about and those he wrote for. But perhaps he was best known for his *On the Road* and *Sunday Morning* television broadcasts. He loved middle America, and he traveled highways and byways to find people and stories that reflected the essence of decency and American spirit. Charles Kuralt died on July 4th, 1997, at the age of 62.

FOR DISCUSSION AND REFLECTION

➤ Why do you think Mr. Misenheimer created and tended the highway garden? (Answers will vary, but he wanted to make the world a better place. He felt it was his duty and wanted to follow his parents' teachings.)

➤ Why did Haeja take over the garden? (She had had a childhood dream about living among flowers and wanted to learn about nature; she was grateful to Mr. Misenheimer for being so important in her life and wanted to keep the garden going in order to pay tribute to him.)

➤ What would have happened if Mr. Misenheimer had never met Haeja? (The park probably would have become overgrown, as he predicted.)

Writing

QUICK ASSESS

Do students' charts:

✔ show understanding of the story?

✔ offer one cause-and-effect sentence of their own?

Remind students to jot "why" and "how" questions as they read the selection. They will complete cause-and-effect charts that are based on the selection.

READING AND WRITING EXTENSIONS

➤ Bring in some landscape paintings and have students sketch their impressions of Mr. Misenheimer's garden in the style of Monet or other French Impressionists.

➤ Read to the class the picture book *Miss Rumphius*, by Barbara Cooney, and have students discuss and compare the goals of Miss Rumphius and Mr. Misenheimer.

Four If...Then...

C r i t i c a l   R e a d i n g

FOCUS

Understanding writing often involves drawing conclusions from general statements.

BACKGROUND

Charles Kuralt takes the reader to a higher level of thinking as he uses the garden metaphor to encourage students to think beyond just planting seeds and growing flowers. He wants the readers to understand that they will reap what they sow, in terms of good deeds in their life. Students may be stimulated to think of "their" reason for being here and the effect of their existence.

➤ Lesson Four focuses on drawing conclusions and moving from general to specific statements. For instance, a general statement could be: "Most seventh graders go on to graduate from high school in five more years." A specific statement would be: "The students in this class are seventh graders." The conclusion statement would be: "Most of the students in this class will probably graduate from high school in five years."

FOR DISCUSSION AND REFLECTION

➤ How does one plant love and kindness? (Anyone can do this by volunteering at school or in the community, being thoughtful and respectful to family and friends, and following the examples set by admirable people.)

➤ What might happen as a result? (You will receive extrinsic and intrinsic rewards; people will admire you for your good deeds and at the same time you will feel better about yourself.)

➤ Why is it important to be able to draw conclusions from "if . . . then . . ." statements? (Answers will vary.)

W r i t i n g

QUICK ASSESS

Are students' conclusions:

✓ appropriate and logical?

✓ based on the general statement?

Students should practice writing statements based on a general statement before they finally draw a personal conclusion. Remember that the students might need to practice orally with some very concrete examples before moving to the exercise.

READING AND WRITING EXTENSIONS

➤ Invite students to write an essay on what they would like to do to leave the world a better place. Have them put their final copies in a class "Planting the Garden" book to share with others.

➤ Ask students to look in the newspaper, in articles or obituaries, for examples of people that have accomplished something notable in their lives. Have them share their findings with classmates.

See also Answer Key, page 119

Five Alike and Unlike

Critical Reading

FOCUS

Recognizing a pattern of comparison and contrast can make it easier to understand the writer's ideas.

BACKGROUND

Maxine Hong Kingston was born in California of Chinese parents in 1940. She taught English in Hawaii before publishing her first book, *The Woman Warrior*, in 1976; it was named one of the top ten nonfiction works of the decade by *Time* in 1979. In "A Sea Worry," she blends legend, history, and autobiography in a genre that is uniquely hers.

➤ Kingston uses a compare-and-contrast pattern effectively in the selection presented in Lesson Five. The Kingston excerpt, written from a mom's point of view, uses comparison and contrast to great advantage with its vivid description of surfing and her parental fears about the sport. The spectator worries, in amazement, about what might go tragically wrong; the athlete, with confidence, enjoys the thrill of looking danger in the eye.

FOR DISCUSSION AND REFLECTION

➤ Why does the author say, "This is no country for middle-aged women"? (The sport is for young, athletic boys. Moms are nervous at the thought of how dangerous surfing is; they would hate to have to go out to rescue anyone.)

➤ What is the surfer's favorite part? (It is being in the middle of the tube, when there is water all around you but you remain dry. Surfers probably also like flirting with danger.)

➤ What does Kingston mean that "surfing is like a religion," and what can you equate to the feeling of the body-surf experience? (This simile describes the devotion and spiritual relationship of the surfer with the waves. Similar experiences might include skateboarding, windsurfing, or skiing.)

Writing

QUICK ASSESS

Do students' conclusions:

✓ explain their viewpoints?

✓ compare their views with Kingston's?

Before they draw one conclusion about Kingston's and the surfers' views of the bodysurfing experience, students are expected to use a Venn diagram to compare and contrast the views of the author with those of the young surfers. Remind them that opposing views and differences go on either side, and that the center, where the circles intersect, is reserved for the ideas that are held in common.

READING AND WRITING EXTENSIONS

➤ Bring in pictures or videos that show actual surfing competitions from Hawaii or California to inspire the students to extend their paragraphs into short stories. Encourage them to draw on facts from research as well as from Kingston's selection.

➤ Have students think about what captivates them the way surfing captivates Kingston's son. Perhaps it is a sport, a hobby, or a favorite place. Encourage them to share their feelings with classmates.

See also Answer Key, page 120

CONFLICT: THE DRIVING FORCE

Unit Overview

In "Conflict: The Driving Force," students will learn about five types of conflict: character vs. character, character vs. self, character vs. destiny, character vs. society, and character vs. nature. As they read and respond to the writing of Cynthia Rylant, Edith Wharton, Mary Whitebird, and Laurence Yep, students will discover how conflict can charge stories with excitement and deliver insights to the reader about the behavior of characters and themselves.

Literature Focus

Lesson	Literature
1. Head to Head	**Cynthia Rylant,** "Shells" (Short Story)
2. Me, Myself, and I	**Cynthia Rylant,** "Shells" (Short Story)
3. The Shape of Destiny	**Edith Wharton,** "Appointment in Baghdad" (Short Story)
4. A Different Drummer	**Mary Whitebird,** from "Ta-Na-E-Ka" (Short Story)
5. Against the Elements	**Laurence Yep,** from *Dragonwings* (Fiction)

Reading Focus

1. Good readers increase their understanding by thinking about conflicts between characters.
2. As you read, watch for internal conflicts that reveal opposing thoughts or feelings within a character.
3. Good readers understand that characters' struggles against destiny are a way to make us examine human nature.
4. Conflicts between characters and society often reveal information about the characters' motivations, values, and personality traits.
5. Critical readers understand that a conflict with nature creates suspense and often reveals characters' personalities.

Writing Focus

1. Write about a story's conflicts and make a prediction about how they might be resolved.
2. Explain how a character resolves his internal conflicts.
3. Write a tale about a character who seeks to change his or her destiny.
4. Offer advice to the narrator of a short story.
5. Explain how a character's actions reveal her personality.

One Head to Head

Critical Reading

FOCUS

Conflict is at the heart of Cynthia Rylant's "Shells":

"They had been living together, the two of them, for six months. Michael's parents had died and only Esther could take him in—or, only she had offered to. Michael's other relatives could not imagine dealing with a fourteen-year-old boy. They wanted peaceful lives."

BACKGROUND

Cynthia Rylant is a contemporary writer whose characters face many issues—issues to which teens are able to relate. Just as real people deal with conflict in their lives, so do Rylant's characters.

➤ Lesson One invites students to focus on a multifaceted conflict between two people—a young teenage boy whose parents have died and his elderly, unmarried aunt, who invites the boy to live with her. Students will be able to see all kinds of possibilities for conflict if they just picture themselves in the same situation.

FOR DISCUSSION AND REFLECTION

➤ What are the conflicts between Michael and Aunt Esther? (The main problems between Michael and Aunt Esther are that Michael's parents have died, he's in a new school and has no friends, he's cooped up in a condo, she doesn't understand teenagers, and she's only taken him in out of loyalty to her family.)

➤ Who is more at fault in this story, Michael or his aunt? (It would seem that they are both at fault. Honesty and communication are at the root of the problem. They talk "at" each other, but neither listens to the other; they blame each other, but they don't try to resolve the issues.)

➤ Do you think Michael really hates his aunt? (He probably thinks he does, but it is more a matter of frustration than hate, because of the situation into which he's been placed.)

Writing

QUICK ASSESS

Do students' responses:

✔ identify the conflicts between Michael and Aunt Esther?

✔ show understanding of how conflict affects characters?

✔ offer a reasonable prediction?

As students reflect on the first part of "Shells" and Michael's reaction to living with his Aunt Esther, they should try to put themselves in the same situation to understand how he feels. Then they need to explain the external conflicts surrounding this relationship and predict how the conflicts might be resolved.

READING AND WRITING EXTENSIONS

➤ Have students write a journal entry for one of the following proverbs and tell how it relates to this story: "Honesty is the best policy" or "Say what you mean and mean what you say."

➤ Invite students to read some of Cynthia Rylant's other works such as the Newbery Honor Book, *A Fine White Dust*, whose narrator is a fourteen-year-old boy, or her autobiography, *But I'll Be Back Again*.

See also Answer Key, page 120

Two Me, Myself, and I

Critical Reading

FOCUS

The reader gains insight from watching characters struggle with internal conflict:

"They leaned their heads over the tank and found him. The crab, finished with the old home that no longer fit, was coming out of his shell."

BACKGROUND

This lesson moves students from external to internal conflict as they focus on the inner struggle in which Michael is engaged. He must face pain and loneliness so that he doesn't continue to shut everyone out of his life, especially his Aunt Esther. Make sure that students realize that internal conflict is that which is "inside," within our minds, not physical, on the "outside" of our bodies. Help students to understand that people, like characters, often face mental struggles in which they wrestle with their consciences or play tug-of-war with an "inner voice."

FOR DISCUSSION AND REFLECTION

➤ What part does the crab play in the story? (Sluggo is a lot like Michael; they both have shells, want companionship, and need to adjust to a new home. Sluggo helps Michael understand that they are both better off without their shells.)

➤ How has Michael grown out of his shell? (He has matured by facing his pain and loneliness and admitting his aunt into his life.)

➤ Does Aunt Esther have any internal conflicts? (Aunt Esther has to deal with her loneliness and her old way of life just as Michael has to deal with his; she has to lose her "shell" just as Sluggo and Michael need to lose theirs.)

➤ What do you think would be the most difficult inner conflict to deal with in the story? (Answers will vary but encourage students to make personal connections to the story.)

➤ What inner conflicts have you struggled to resolve? (Responses will vary. Even if students don't wish to share this personal information, encourage them to reflect on the topic privately.)

Writing

QUICK ASSESS

Do students' paragraphs:

✓ recognize examples of inner conflict from the story?

✓ discuss how Michael resolved his inner conflict?

Students will write their impressions of the story's ending and then list different internal conflicts that Michael experiences. As they explain which of Michael's conflicts have been resolved, remind them to use examples from the story as support.

READING AND WRITING EXTENSIONS

➤ Have students write an epilogue that takes place four to five years in the future. Suggest that they think again about the resolution of conflicts in the second part of the story before they start to write.

➤ Discuss together the meaning of the phrase "the old home that no longer fit," and have students write about how its meaning might connect to their own lives.

See also Answer Key, page 121

Three The Shape of Destiny

C r i t i c a l   R e a d i n g

FOCUS

In Edith Wharton's "Appointment in Baghdad," an unsuspecting character comes face to face with destiny:

"There is little time! I must fly at once to Baghdad!"

BACKGROUND

"Appointment in Baghdad" reminds readers that they don't always have control over their own destiny. Help students to understand the idea of destiny by talking about the experience of driving a car. Even though people obey all of the traffic laws, remain alert, and focus on everything around them, they might still be rear-ended at the stoplight. As hard as people sometimes try to control their circumstances, things happen that cannot be prevented.

➤ Lesson Three examines the conflict of character versus destiny. Edith Wharton's young man struggles to avoid his own death. Students should enjoy watching him trying to outwit his inevitable destiny, only to be snared by the ensuing struggle. It's important that the students try to imagine what change of circumstances would affect the outcome, thus deepening their involvement with the characters. It's challenging for students to reflect on how the characters play the cards that they've been dealt, whether they accept their fate or attempt to change it.

➤ Point out how students might tamper with the details of the story to change the outcome by trying "What if" questions. For instance, "What if the horse and rider get lost on their way to Baghdad?" or "What if the rider changes his mind and returns?"

FOR DISCUSSION AND REFLECTION

➤ Is the title of the story a good one? Why or why not? (Have students consider the implications of the word *appointment*, especially in contrast to a word like *meeting*.)

➤ Is there any way that the assistant's destiny could have been changed? (Responses will vary. Death is a foregone conclusion, but do we have some impact on the time and place?)

➤ Were you surprised by the ending? Explain. (Answers will vary.)

W r i t i n g

QUICK ASSESS

Do students' tales:

✓ use conflict effectively?

✓ feature a character attempting to change his or her destiny?

After the students predict a different ending to Wharton's story, they are asked to write a short tale about how someone might change destiny in his or her own life. Remind them to keep conflict in their story in order to keep it suspenseful.

READING AND WRITING EXTENSIONS

➤ Have students read some Native American legends or familiar folk or fairy tales. Then have them discuss the main characters' struggle against their destiny.

➤ Ask students to locate Baghdad on a map, research it on the Internet, and share the information with the class.

Four A Different Drummer

Critical Reading

FOCUS

Characters sometimes feel in conflict with their society and its values and expectations.

BACKGROUND

In "A Different Drummer," students have an opportunity to focus on another kind of conflict, the struggle between character and society. Before they read the excerpt from Mary Whitebird's "Ta-Na-E-Ka," students may need help thinking of situations in which they themselves have felt a conflict with societal or cultural expectations.

➤ Brainstorm with students a list of possible conflicts between individuals and society. Include issues and situations relating to gender roles, religious beliefs, experiences with other cultures, unfair laws, established family customs, and so on. Students may enjoy making connections to familiar literary characters or works that involve societal conflict—perhaps *Huckleberry Finn* or *Romeo and Juliet*.

➤ Students who enjoy reading this selection might be encouraged to read selections from *4 Winds: Poems from Indian Rituals* by Gene Meany Hodge or *The Lone Ranger and Tonto Fistfight in Heaven* by Sherman Alexie.

FOR DISCUSSION AND REFLECTION

➤ What kind of girl is the narrator? (Responses will vary but should make note of her knowledge of her Indian heritage and her grandfather's life, her questioning of the Ta-Na-E-Ka ritual, her willingness to protest to her mother and complain to her teacher, her fondness for school, and her desire for a life of excitement.)

➤ In what rituals have you participated? Were there times when you felt you didn't fit in? (Responses will vary.)

Writing

QUICK ASSESS

Do students' letters:

✓ show understanding of the conflict?

✓ offer advice about possible resolutions?

After writing about personal experiences in which they "heard a different drummer," students are asked to write a letter explaining how Whitebird's narrator might resolve her conflict. Have several students read their letters aloud.

READING AND WRITING EXTENSIONS

➤ Have students imagine they are either the female narrator or Roger Deer Leg, her cousin, who wants to be an accountant. Invite them to write a letter to their parents explaining their feelings about the Ta-Na-E-Ka ceremony.

➤ Have students write a poem about a time when they felt at odds with social or cultural expectations. Encourage them to read their works to the class.

See also Answer Key, page 121

Five Against the Elements

Critical Reading

FOCUS

A character's actions in a battle with nature reveal his or her personality.

BACKGROUND

Laurence Yep, a Chinese American, felt isolated and alienated growing up. He draws from his own experience to portray Moonshadow and his father, Windrider, in *Dragonwings*, a Newbery Honor winner. The excerpt in this lesson provides students with a good example of a character's struggle against nature.

➤ The great 1906 San Francisco earthquake, which ranks as one of the most significant earthquakes of all time, lasted some 45 to 60 seconds and was felt from southern Oregon to south of Los Angeles and as far inland as central Nevada. Shaking damage and fire ravaged the city and caused between 2,100 and 2,800 fatalities. As Yep's writing shows, the desperation of being involved in such a quake is counteracted by the fortitude and unselfish nature of the characters. For example, Miss Whitlaw says, "We must get those people out . . . . After all, we were put on this earth to help one another."

FOR DISCUSSION AND REFLECTION

➤ Where do you see the father's character traits emerge? (He shows compassion by trying to rescue the victims; he shows a sense of humor with his notice of Miss Whitlaw's nightgown; he seems absentminded or distracted when he puts his boots on the wrong feet, and so on.)

➤ What kinds of problems has the earthquake created in the city? (Housing has been destroyed, gas lines and water mains are broken, people are trapped under rubble, fires have started, and lives have been lost.)

➤ Do you think people had any warning or were they surprised by the quake? (The state that the survivors are in tells the reader that they were caught unaware. For instance, people are in nightclothes or almost naked, wandering about, and carrying things not appropriate for a disaster.)

Writing

QUICK ASSESS

Do students' responses:

✓ focus on actions that reveal Miss Whitlaw's character?

✓ include text details as support?

Help students to find details that describe and reveal Miss Whitlaw's character by encouraging them to look in the text for clues about her actions. Recommend that they begin their sentences with "I think Miss Whitlaw is very determined because . . . ."

READING AND WRITING EXTENSIONS

➤ Have students read and share their impressions of excerpts from Howard Fast's historical fiction novel *The Immigrants*, which begins with the shattering scene of San Francisco's earthquake in 1906.

➤ Have students find human-interest stories in the newspaper about people's battles with nature and share oral summaries of them with the class.

See also Answer Key, page 121

Unit Overview

In this unit, students explore authors' various choices about structure and styles of writing. As they read works by Jack London, Scott O'Dell, Wing Tek Lum, Anton Chekhov, and Alonzo Lopez, students will deepen their understanding of how an author might select a certain structure to enhance a message and begin to develop a personal style of their own.

Literature Focus

	Lesson	Literature
1.	What Makes a Style?	**Jack London,** from *The Call of the Wild* (Fiction)
		Scott O'Dell, from *Island of the Blue Dolphins* (Fiction)
2.	A Poetic Style	**Wing Tek Lum,** "Chinese Hot Pot" (Poetry)
3.	Dramatic Structure	**Anton Chekhov,** *The Inspector-General* (Drama)
4.	How to Build a Poem	**Alonzo Lopez,** "Direction" (Poetry)
5.	Finding a Style and Structure	

Reading Focus

1. A writer makes choices about how to express ideas. These choices—about word choice, sentence length, and so on—make up the author's style.
2. The style an author uses can reflect how the author feels about the subject.
3. A drama has a distinctive structure, which includes stage directions and character names set aside from the dialogue.
4. As you read a poem, examine its structure to figure out the reasons behind the writer's placement of words, lines, and stanzas.
5. Choose a style and structure for your own writing that will best reflect your feelings about the subject.

Writing Focus

1. Recommend a novel, based in part on its style.
2. Write an original poem, expressing your feelings about America.
3. Compare in a Venn diagram the structure of dramas and short stories.
4. Write a poem about advice you have received.
5. Write again about an incident, using a different style and structure, and speculate on how a reader might react to it.

One What Makes a Style?

Critical Reading

FOCUS

An author's style is his or her unique way of using language to express ideas.

BACKGROUND

Writers write what they know and are. Not only does an author's background influence *what* is written about, it also influences *how* it is written. Style is a reflection not only of the author, but the time in which he or she lives and the audience for whom he or she writes. Remind students that a writer's style includes word choice, tone, point of view, sentence length, and use of figurative language.

➤ The two adventure stories presented in Lesson One provide excellent examples of two very different styles of a single genre. Jack London, who wrote at the turn of the century, used his explorations in the Yukon as background for his stories written in an elaborate, formal style. He uses a lot of difficult vocabulary that students will need to conquer. Reading his work is labor intensive—like the slow, careful trudging through the deep snow about which London writes.

➤ The reading level of Scott O'Dell's piece is less difficult and easier to read than that of London. Help students to see how O'Dell's more informal style is at least partially a product of more contemporary times. Reading the selections aloud with students gives them a better sense of the authors' styles, and once students read both selections it will be an interesting process to discuss their differences.

FOR DISCUSSION AND REFLECTION

➤ Which excerpt was easier to read and why? (O'Dell's informal piece is probably easier to read, with shorter sentences, lighter tone, and less difficult vocabulary.)

➤ What kind of figurative language does Scott O'Dell use? (Responses will vary. Students may note that he uses personification, such as the waves making "angry" noises or sounding like "people laughing" and the simile comparing the path of the canoe to a snake.)

Writing

QUICK ASSESS

Do students' responses:

✓ recommend one book?

✓ provide adequate reasons?

✓ discuss style?

Suggest that students mark their text with different colors for the various style attributes. Once the students have filled in the chart of style attributes, they will recommend which book should be a required novel selection. Students need to use good topic sentences, with support details taken from their attribute chart.

READING AND WRITING EXTENSIONS

➤ Have students research Jack London or Scott O'Dell for more background information about their lives and share their findings with the class.

➤ Have students visualize the two excerpts, share their impressions orally, and then turn their visualizations into a sketch that reflects the two scenes.

See also Answer Key, page 121

TWO A Poetic Style

Critical Reading

FOCUS

Our style reveals who we are and what we think:

"My dream of America is like dá bìn lóuh . . . ."

BACKGROUND

Instead of telling a story or sharing a thought with long prose passages, poetry is a genre that does the work of a video camera. The poet's world touches the reader with fleeting thoughts and impressions; figurative language and sound appeal to one's senses and feelings. Because of the uniqueness of poetry, this genre's brevity forces the poet to make precise word choices, like a stone mason picking each rock for a chimney or an artist cutting each piece of glass for an intricate window. Each piece must be a perfect fit. It is with the same, careful consideration that the poet chooses words.

➤ This lesson invites students to examine the metaphoric style of Wing Tek Lum. "Chinese Hot Pot" is an excellent example of a poetic style that uses figurative language and imagery to make the reader see something in a new light. (For instance, the image of sharing the pot and the fire shows cooperation and friendship. The variety of foods is a symbol for different ethnic groups all being combined as Americans.)

FOR DISCUSSION AND REFLECTION

➤ What makes Lum's style distinctive in "Chinese Hot Pot"? (Responses may include the simple but meaningful word choice, the short lines with no punctuation at the ends, or the simile about stew.)

➤ What impression does Lum's poem give and what are the clues? (America is a good place; he likes it because there is freedom and choice and happiness. Clues include words like "common pot," "chooses what he wishes," "all in one broth," "shared," and "sweet.")

➤ What simile does Lum use as the basic idea of his poem? (His simile is based on the idea that a stew has a lot of different ingredients, just like America has a lot of mixtures and choices.)

Writing

QUICK ASSESS

Do students' poems:

✓ imitate Lum's style?

✓ express a feeling about America?

✓ reflect careful word choice?

Once students have worked through the style checklist, they will write a poem, imitating Lum's style, to share their personal impressions of America.

READING AND WRITING EXTENSIONS

➤ Have students work together to create a class "cookbook" of "America is . . . ." poems. Some students could write the poems, and others could draw illustrations to accompany them.

➤ Have students read another poem that uses a metaphor or a simile in its structure—"America is" by Langston Hughes or "Pigeon Woman" by May Swenson.

Three Dramatic Structure

Critical Reading

FOCUS

Anton Chekhov's *The Inspector-General* illustrates how dramatic structure differs from a short story:

"The curtain goes up to reveal falling snow and a cart facing away from us. Enter the STORYTELLER, who begins to read the story."

BACKGROUND

Whether you have front row seats for opening night at the Globe, balcony tickets for Broadway, or lawn chair seats for a play by the kids in the neighborhood, there's something exciting about seeing a live performance on the stage. Playwright and short story writer, Anton Chekhov, whose successes include *The Seagull, Three Sisters*, and *The Cherry Orchard*, was born in Russia in 1860 and died of a heart attack in 1904.

➤ As they read *The Inspector-General*, students should quickly notice that the drama has all the necessary elements of a short story, such as setting, plot, and characters; however, it also has stage directions for crew and performers written in parentheses, as well as dialogue that is written as script. For instance, stage directions for the storyteller to exit are in parentheses at the end of his speech. Be sure that students understand that different character parts are written in bold capital letters, and the acting directions are also in parentheses.

FOR DISCUSSION AND REFLECTION

➤ What elements do dramas and short stories have in common? (They both have setting, characters, plot, conflict, and climax.)

➤ How do dramas and short stories differ? (Dramas have a script for characters' dialogue, stage directions for the crew and performers, props, sound effects, and acts and scenes.)

➤ What do you think of Chekhov's ending? (Responses will vary. Students may enjoy the suspense of wondering if the characters are aware of each other and if their dialogue is just a coincidence to make readers think they know of each other's identity.)

Writing

QUICK ASSESS

Do students' Venn diagrams:

✔ show similarities between the structure of the two genres?

✔ show differences between the structure of the two genres?

Students should review their response notes to look for clues in the play that hint that the driver and the traveler are aware of each other before completing the Venn diagram about the elements of dramas and short stories.

READING AND WRITING EXTENSIONS

➤ Have students rehearse and perform *The Inspector-General* for another class or grade level.

➤ Invite students to write a short one-act play about a time when they wanted to keep their identity hidden or a time when they were misidentified as someone else. Encourage them to include stage directions in their scripts and to form small groups to read through their creations.

See also Answer Key, page 122

Four How to Build a Poem

Critical Reading

FOCUS

In free verse poems writers make up their own rules of structure.

BACKGROUND

Lesson Four gives students an opportunity to explore the structure of Alonzo Lopez's poem "Direction." They will need to figure out how message and structure go hand in hand to complement each other. Once students discuss how they feel about the poem, you might call their attention to why the poet wrote the poem the way he did. What other options might there be? How else could Lopez call attention to the things he learned from his grandfather?

➤ Remind students that often the poet uses patterns of words that appeal to the reader's senses and imagination and that the theme of the poem is meant to touch the reader's mind.

➤ Often, the poem is shaped to fit a prescribed format—like a template or formula—that the poet follows for the finished product (such as sonnets, narratives, concrete poems, diamantes, or haiku). On the other hand, a poet may favor free verse and make up the rules as he or she goes along. The structure will depend on the whim of the writer; and the final product will reflect the subject matter and the impression that the poet wants to leave with the reader.

FOR DISCUSSION AND REFLECTION

➤ Why is the poem called "Direction"? (Responses will vary. Students may say that each direction has something different to offer, like enjoying different scenery on different highways. A full life would include many directions. Also, remind students that giving directions can mean giving advice.)

➤ Why has the poet used comparisons to animals? Does it reveal anything about him? (We make associations with these animals, and as a Native American, Lopez felt that the laws of nature give guidance and "direction" in life.)

➤ Who has given you good advice? (Responses will vary, but hearing what others say may help students choose their own topics.)

Writing

QUICK ASSESS

Do the students' poems:

✓ reflect the style and structure of "Direction"?

✓ describe advice that was offered?

Once students have discussed the structure of Alonzo Lopez's "Direction," they will be prepared to use it as a model for their own poems about a time when someone important to them offered advice.

READING AND WRITING EXTENSIONS

➤ Have students create a new structure for Lopez's lines. Invite them to change the order of lines, regroup them, or use white space in creative ways—perhaps as a map or a compass rose. Have the new versions displayed for all to see.

➤ Have students look at the work of other poets to learn more about free verse poetry—perhaps favorites such as Shel Silverstein, Ogden Nash, or E. E. Cummings.

Five Finding a Style and Structure

Critical Reading

FOCUS

Every author's message is influenced by the unique structure and style of the writing.

BACKGROUND

In "Finding a Style and Structure," students should be encouraged to think about how different genres suit different purposes. Talk with them about the different ways they might routinely choose to convey a message—in a formal letter, in a phone call, in an e-mail, in an editorial, and so on. Help them understand how sometimes a purpose can be fulfilled by using more than one genre. It might be helpful here to have them think about how film and book versions of the same story differ. Students need to understand that the style and structure of a piece can provide clues to the author's intent.

➤ Because students often find poetry difficult to understand or appreciate, you might want to spend extra time discussing this genre and its unique characteristics. Encourage students to see that we not only read poems for enjoyment of language and sound, but we also read poetry to untangle the webs of thoughts that the poet feels are important enough to share. Poems amuse and teach; they mystify, tease, and entertain.

FOR DISCUSSION AND REFLECTION

➤ Ask students about the different reasons they might prefer to write a letter to someone instead of communicating by e-mail or telephone.

➤ Which structure is the most difficult for you to write? (Answers will vary, but students might think poetry is the most difficult. Even though poems are short, they may not be easy to write. For students, the easiest form might be a personal note or letter, since they use this format a lot when corresponding with friends.)

➤ Invite students to think about and discover film versions of writings they may have read, such as the 1996 film of *Romeo and Juliet*, starring Leonardo DiCaprio and Clare Danes. Which do they like better? Why?

Writing

QUICK ASSESS

Do students' responses:

✓ describe the incident using new style and structure?

✓ comment on how the new form might affect readers?

You might have the class brainstorm a list of different styles and structures they could use as they write about receiving advice a second time—letters, journals, speeches, phone conversations, instructions, recipes, scenarios, news articles, and so on.

READING AND WRITING EXTENSIONS

➤ Rewrite Alonzo Lopez's "Direction" as a monologue spoken by the grandfather.

➤ Have students transform their "advice" poem into a greeting card with pictures or computer-generated artwork. Some might want to send it to the person who gave them the advice.

Unit Overview

In this unit, students read and respond to poems by Gordon Parks, John Kieran, Edgar Allan Poe, Gwendolyn Brooks, and Paul Fleischman. They will have the opportunity to explore a variety of strategies that poets use to transform language into sound messages with different meanings for different readers and to practice writing poems themselves.

Literature Focus

Lesson	Literature
1. What's It All Mean?	**Gordon Parks,** "The Funeral" (Poetry)
2. Bringing Yourself to a Poem	**John Kieran,** "There's This That I Like About Hockey, My Lad" (Poetry)
3. How a Poem Sounds	**Edgar Allan Poe,** "Annabel Lee" (Poetry)
4. Sound Effects	**Gwendolyn Brooks,** "Cynthia in the Snow" (Poetry)
5. A Figure of Speech	**Paul Fleischman,** "Chrysalis Diary" (Poetry)

Reading Focus

1. Use active reading strategies like restating ideas in your own words and figuring out what images mean. These will help you understand the ideas in a poem.

2. When you read a poem, think about your personal response to it. Connecting to the poem will help you better understand and enjoy it.

3. Use the sound devices you encounter in poetry to determine what ideas the writer is trying to emphasize.

4. Writers use onomatopoeia to create precise images and dramatic sound effects in poetry.

5. Poets often use personification to present unfamiliar ideas in familiar ways.

Writing Focus

1. Complete a chart about two different points of view in a poem.

2. Answer questions about a poem.

3. Rewrite a poem in a different form and compare the new version to the original.

4. Write a poem about a place using onomatopoeia to describe the noises you heard.

5. Personify a textbook topic in an original poem.

One What's It All Mean?

Critical Reading

FOCUS

Reading a poem carefully will help the reader find clues to its meaning.

BACKGROUND

Gordon Parks, a best-selling and award-winning photographer, creates word pictures in "The Funeral." Just the title alone will put many images in the students' minds prior to reading the poem, based on their personal experiences with funerals. Discuss how funerals may involve a "return" of a physical and mental nature—perhaps to one's roots—as well as a review of the memories and feelings associated with the deceased. Be sure to help students see how Parks uses vivid verbs and descriptors to conjure up very strong mental pictures for the reader, pictures that allow us to share the emotions he himself is feeling.

➤ Explain that in this lesson, students are on a scavenger hunt for clues that will tell Parks's story and give them insights about the differences between a child's and adult's view of the past. For instance, we always see things looming much larger as children than the reality we notice as adults: "Time had whittled down to mere hills / The great mountains of my childhood," or "raging rivers" become "gentle streams." The father was probably no "giant," but he seemed larger than life to a young child.

FOR DISCUSSION AND REFLECTION

➤ What can you infer from the poem about the relationship of the father and child? ("A hundred strong men strained . . . ." or "Only the giant who was my father . . . ." or the fact that he wrote the poem at all point out reverence.)

➤ What idea is Gordon Parks trying to share with us? (Possible meanings include that nothing stays the same, love for family doesn't diminish, the passage of time affects our memories, you can't ever go back, and other similar answers. Students need to realize that there may be more than one correct response.)

Writing

QUICK ASSESS

Do students' charts:

✓ restate the main ideas and feelings contained in the poem?

✓ show understanding of the young and old perspective?

Once students have read and reread the poem, they need to visualize the meanings and search line by line for words and phrases that create images and give hints about the message the author wants us to receive. Filling in the idea chart will help them see the contrasts between the young and the old perspective in the poem.

READING AND WRITING EXTENSIONS

➤ Ask students to find examples of paintings, photography, and music that would be appropriate accompaniments to "The Funeral." Ansel Adams's work might be a good suggestion.

➤ Have students write a journal entry about the father from the point of view of the one returning for the funeral.

See also Answer Key, page 122

Two Bringing Yourself to a Poem

C r i t i c a l   R e a d i n g

FOCUS
Poetry offers readers a chance to judge and connect on a personal level:

"There's this that I like about hockey, my lad; It's a clattering, battering sport."

BACKGROUND

With the right combination of writer's clues and reader's connections, poems can be simultaneously insightful and mystifying. Poetry not only demands us to conduct several readings, it implores us to read it aloud. Rhyme and rhythm make John Kieran's poem fun to read aloud. Students will love the opportunity to "be on stage" and bring a poem to life.

➤ As students read "There's This That I Like About Hockey, My Lad," they will have the opportunity to decipher the poet's clues about himself. You may want to tell them that Kieran is the author of a 520-page book about the Olympics and one called *The American Sporting Scene*. Some students may want to bring their own skating or sports experiences to the page as well. So many students play ice hockey, field hockey, football, or soccer that they should have no trouble relating to the love of a rough and challenging sports contest.

FOR DISCUSSION AND REFLECTION

➤ What can you infer about the speaker in this selection? (Accept a variety of responses. He may be Irish or English because of the words "lad and chap." He is probably a hockey fan because he knows about the game, and he sees enjoyment in the challenge of a very rough, competitive sport.)

➤ What metaphor is used in the poem to show the roughness of the sport? (Kieran uses military connotations with words like "fort," "deploy," "to maul and to maim," "fight," and "enemy," all suggesting that hockey is a war.)

➤ Does the speaker like hockey, even though it's rough? (Students will probably answer that he does. He uses words like "this that I like," "popular pastime," "rollicking game," and "And ho! . . . And hey! for a glorious night.")

➤ Why does the author repeat most of the first line of each stanza three times? (He wants to emphasize his feelings about the game; even though it's rough and dangerous, the thrill is in the contest.)

W r i t i n g

QUICK ASSESS
Do students' responses:

✓ show a thoughtful reading of the poem?

✓ answer two questions?

As students answer questions about the poem, be sure that they draw on specific words and phrases to support their ideas.

READING AND WRITING EXTENSIONS

➤ Invite students to write an original poem about their favorite team sport. They might brainstorm some of the moves and feelings that they associate with the sport before they begin.

➤ Ask students to look for articles in the newspaper about hockey and other sports with lots of body contact. Have them look for and discuss word choice and imagery that focuses on the sport's roughness.

Three How a Poem Sounds

Critical Reading

FOCUS

Rhyme, rhythm, and repetition are key elements of "Annabel Lee":

"*I* was a child and *she* was a child, / In this kingdom by the sea: / But we loved with a love that was more than love—I and my Annabel Lee—...."

BACKGROUND

Edgar Allan Poe, usually associated with the horror genre, is also famous for his poems. An important author of the nineteenth century, Poe wrote in a marvelous style that mirrored his dark, erratic life. He married his thirteen-year-old cousin, who died of tuberculosis; he missed her terribly and only lived two more years, dying at the age of forty. There has been much controversy surrounding his death, and it's now believed that perhaps his early demise was the result of rabies rather than alcoholism, as had been previously suspected.

➤ "Annabel Lee" is a tribute to Poe's young wife after her death. Rather than striking a melancholy note, it almost seems upbeat and optimistic with its repeating rhymes and sing-song rhythm. The speaker blames the angels (who were jealous of the love he and Annabel Lee had together) for coming down and "chilling and killing" his Annabel Lee. Even though she's left him in body, he holds onto her spirit, down by the sea.

FOR DISCUSSION AND REFLECTION

➤ Where and why does Poe use repetition? (Examples include "I and my Annabel Lee," "My beautiful Annabel Lee," "Of the beautiful Annabel Lee," "Of my darling—my darling," and "in this kingdom by the sea." The repetition emphasizes the speaker's feelings and makes him sound pleading and forlorn, as if he can't believe his love is really gone.)

➤ Why do you think Poe says the angels were envious and covetous of them? (Students may answer that perhaps it shows that the love was so intense that it made others jealous.)

➤ What are "highborn kinsmen"? (They are the angels with whom Annabel Lee now resides.)

➤ How depressing is this poem? (Responses will vary. Poe's beautiful images of angels and moonbeams and stars may make some readers feel better about Annabel Lee's death.)

Writing

QUICK ASSESS

Do students' responses:

✓ capture the essence of the poem in another form?

✓ compare their writing to the poem?

Once they rate the poem on its sound devices, students will rewrite the sentiments of the poem in another form. They will probably reach the conclusion that the poem is more effective in expressing one's feelings.

READING AND WRITING EXTENSIONS

➤ Have students write their own poems about a person they know well using Poe's "Annabel Lee" as a model. Invite them to employ sound devices such as rhyme and repetition in each stanza.

➤ Encourage students to read some of Poe's short stories, such as "The Tell-Tale Heart," to see the darker side of his writing.

See also Answer Key, page 123

Four Sound Effects

Critical Reading

FOCUS

Onomatopoeia is used to create strong, sensory images:

"It SHUSHES. / It hushes / The loudness in the road."

BACKGROUND

The focus of this lesson is learning about onomatopoeia, words that sound like sounds. For instance, the sound a dog makes is "ruff" or "grrrrr," while a cat might say "meow." If the perpetrator hits his victim over the head with a club, it might sound like "thunk," or the sound of a home run at the ballgame might be a loud "crack."

➤ Help students to see that we can write the sounds we hear phonetically and use them to enhance our writing. They appeal to the senses of the reader and lend drama to poetry as well as prose. Following the reading aloud of Gwendolyn Brooks's poem, students may want to try to write lines that describe other sounds that falling snow might make.

FOR DISCUSSION AND REFLECTION

➤ What kinds of writers and speakers often use onomatopoeia and why? (Answers may vary, but some examples would be sports commentators, short story writers, music critics, and others, to make their writing more colorful, meaningful, and exciting.)

➤ Why are sound effects important to the poem, "Cynthia in the Snow"? (Responses will vary.)

➤ What is your favorite line from the poem? (Answers will vary, but you should ask students to explain their choices.)

Writing

QUICK ASSESS

Do students' poems:

✓ illustrate a variety of noises?

✓ use onomatopoeia effectively?

Before students write their own onomatopoetic poem about a special place, it would be helpful if they jot down the noises first in a list. Remind them that their goal is not a story, but a quick impression of sound that can rhyme or be in free verse. If their work is in prose to start with, they will need to pull out words to make it into shorter, quicker thoughts. They need to create their own poetic structure and stick to it.

READING AND WRITING EXTENSIONS

➤ Make arrangements to take the students on a field trip, to a concert, or to a play that would relate to the topic of sound. Perhaps you could play the soundtrack from *Stomp* or *Riverdance*. Have students write about their impressions of what they hear.

➤ Ask students to select another weather-related subject (such as heat, rain, wind, ice melting, or flooding) and describe it in a single sentence using onomatopoeia. Have students read their descriptions aloud, experimenting with different tones of voice.

Five A Figure of Speech

Critical Reading

FOCUS

Personification is a technique in which nonhuman things are given human characteristics, as when a chrysalis says:

"I feel immeasurably alone."

BACKGROUND

As you begin this lesson, remind students that figurative language allows readers to see familiar things in fresh, new ways, moving their brains from a concrete to a more abstract or imaginative level of thinking. Paul Fleischman employs beautiful figurative language in his poems. Fleischman aims his work at the young adult audience, using poetry as a stimulus for interesting them in science. Students may agree that textbook topics, when put into poems, become more comprehensible and "user friendly" rather than intimidating scientific language.

➤ Fleischman's poem about a chrysalis making the transition into a butterfly is a topic that often seems difficult to understand from a scientific point of view, but a chrysalis with human characteristics gives a whole new meaning to the process. Each phase is written as a diary entry and can be compared to the actual scientific change that occurs in the transformation.

FOR DISCUSSION AND REFLECTION

➤ What human qualities does Fleischman give the chrysalis? (It thinks, studies, hears, writes, sees, and so on.)

➤ Why does the poet use a journal for the format of the poem? (One possible response is because the metamorphosis takes place in stages, and the diary moves us through a time sequence.)

➤ What other natural phenomena are described in this poem? (Answers may include leaves, wind, snow, day and night, an ice storm, and green buds on trees of spring.)

➤ How does the poem's ending make you feel about the chrysalis? (Answers may include that it is happy in the end as it smells the breeze and recalls a dream of flying, going from the death of winter to the rebirth of spring.)

Writing

QUICK ASSESS

Do students' poems:

✔ use appropriate textbook topics?

✔ show understanding of personification?

After students record examples of personification from the poem in their webs, they will use topics from their social studies or science classes to personify in an original poem.

READING AND WRITING EXTENSIONS

➤ Help students compare the process of metamorphosis with the poetic account by inviting a science expert to speak to the students and to bring some examples of the chrysalis in its different stages.

➤ Have students draw the chrysalis at one stage as described in Fleischman's poem, trying to capture its feelings.

See also Answer Key, page 123

PERSUASIVE WRITING

Unit Overview

In the unit "Active Reading: Persuasive Writing," students will study and practice several techniques used by persuasive writers to build sturdy arguments: stating a clear opinion, using facts as support, choosing words to appeal to their readers' emotions, and selecting an effective tone. As they read nonfiction by Marc H. Morial, Roger Ebert, and Anna Quindlen, students will learn how persuasive writing appeals to both the intellect and the emotions.

Literature Focus

Lesson	Literature
1. The Viewpoint	**Marc H. Morial,** "Our Juvenile Curfew Is Working" (Nonfiction)
2. The Support	
3. The Language	**Roger Ebert,** from *"Titanic"* (Nonfiction)
4. The Emotional Appeal	**Anna Quindlen,** "Homeless" (Nonfiction)
5. The Tone	**Anna Quindlen,** "Homeless" (Nonfiction)

Reading Focus

1. When you evaluate a piece of persuasive writing, start by identifying the author's viewpoint.
2. When you read persuasive writing, look for facts that support the author's opinion.
3. Persuasive writers use loaded words in order to make their arguments more effective.
4. Persuasive writers often tell stories or give examples designed to appeal to our emotions.
5. In a persuasive piece, the writer's tone will give you strong clues about how you, the reader, are supposed to feel.

Writing Focus

1. Write a short letter to the author, explaining your reaction to his viewpoint.
2. Write a paragraph expressing your opinion on an issue of your choosing.
3. Explain whether an author's use of loaded words makes his movie review effective.
4. Explain whether a writer's emotional appeal was effective.
5. Analyze the tone of an essay.

One The Viewpoint

C r i t i c a l   R e a d i n g

BACKGROUND

Begin this unit by discussing with students the importance of being on a constant lookout for clues about who is writing and for what purpose. The *who* and the *why* will have a direct effect on the *what* being used in the argument.

➤ Lesson One introduces students to the topic of an author's viewpoint in persuasive writing. The persuasive argument by Marc H. Morial offers a one-sided argument in favor of a juvenile curfew law.

➤ Mayor Morial sounds genuinely interested in the safety of the city and its population when he says that he needs the community's involvement in order to solve the problem together. He also is persuasive because he offers several creative solutions, such as involving the parents and providing summer camps, swimming pools, and jobs for young people. His many statistics, such as juvenile crime decreasing by 38 percent with the curfew in place, substantiate that progress is being made.

FOR DISCUSSION AND REFLECTION

➤ Discuss with students Morial's viewpoint on the issue of juvenile curfew. Why would the mayor be interested in writing a persuasive essay on this topic? (Students may suggest that perhaps he is running for reelection and wants his successes to stay fresh in the voters' minds.)

➤ Do you agree or disagree with the mayor's argument? Explain. (Answers will vary, but teens may think a curfew is unfair and that their parents would probably like it.)

➤ List some other people who might have similar or different viewpoints on this same issue. (Answers will vary, but people who may agree could be parents, law enforcement and city officials, and business and property owners.)

W r i t i n g

After students identify Morial's perspective on teen curfew, they will write him a letter that expresses their opinion on this subject. Remind them that a letter free of errors and written in correct form using facts as support will make a stronger impression on the mayor than one that is poorly written, using only opinions.

READING AND WRITING EXTENSIONS

➤ Have students investigate whether or not their city or town has any curfew laws for teenagers. Students may organize a panel of different people (such as teens, businesspeople, parents, or police) to discuss how they feel about whatever curfew law is currently in place.

➤ Bring in several editorials from newspapers and magazines and have students practice identifying the author's viewpoint.

See also Answer Key, page 123

Two The Support

Critical Reading

FOCUS

Effective persuasive writers use facts to support their opinion:

"…statistics prove our curfew is working."

BACKGROUND

Lesson Two focuses students' attention on the use of facts to support opinions in persuasive writing.

➤ Students should understand that a balance of fact and opinion is important in an argument. As long as writers use information that can be proved to support their opinion, then their viewpoint can be validated.

➤ It is important to identify the author's viewpoint first and then to identify the pertinent facts that support this opinion. Students should practice distinguishing facts from opinions in Morial's argument, but they may need extra help with this exercise. It's important to point out to students that all of the major facts in the essay (such as times, decreases, increases, and percentages) are numerical statistics that can be proved. Once students learn to sift out facts from opinions, they will be on their way to panning the gold nuggets out of persuasive writing.

FOR DISCUSSION AND REFLECTION

➤ What is the author's opinion on crime in the city of New Orleans? (He feels it is an enormous problem—out of hand and ruining the city.)

➤ What are some of Morial's solutions? (Answers include that youth under the age of 17 must be off the streets between the hours of 8 p.m. to 6 a.m. Sunday through Thursday and from 11 p.m. to 6 a.m. Friday and Saturday; that both juveniles and parents should be held accountable; that there are fines for repeat offenders, and so on.)

➤ List some of the facts Morial uses to show his plan is working. (Answers may include a decrease in juvenile and overall crime, increased feelings of security at home and on the streets, children safer going to school, and families more responsive to their communities.)

Writing

QUICK ASSESS

Do students' paragraphs:

✔ focus on an appropriate issue?

✔ express their opinion on an issue?

✔ include supporting facts?

Students will gain practice distinguishing between fact and opinion by marking their text with red and blue pens before they think of a controversial issue in their own community.

READING AND WRITING EXTENSIONS

➤ Invite students to role-play a "Town Forum" format, with different citizens taking different viewpoints on the topic of teen curfews.

➤ Have the class brainstorm controversial topics in your school. Then, in small groups, ask students to outline a two-sided argument paper in which they express both sides of the issue with supporting facts and statistics and offer a compromise plan of action.

Three **The Language**

C r i t i c a l   R e a d i n g

FOCUS

Roger Ebert's loaded words convey a "thumbs up" review for the movie *Titanic*:

"It is flawlessly crafted, intelligently constructed, strongly acted and spellbinding."

BACKGROUND

A good way for students to become familiar with loaded words is to watch a sports broadcaster on TV or to read a sports column in the newspaper. It becomes obvious very quickly which team the reporter favors. Restaurant guides, travel brochures, advertisements, and editorials are other good examples of writing that would include language aimed at convincing the reader with loaded words.

➤ Most students will be familiar with Roger Ebert's movie reviews either from the newspaper or television, and they will know about his and Gene Siskel's thumbs-up or thumbs-down rating system.

➤ It is obvious from the loaded words in Lesson Three's review that Ebert liked this movie and is giving it a favorable rating. If readers haven't already seen the Oscar-winning film, Ebert's vivid, descriptive language encourages them to. His use of superlatives make the film seem larger than life, a "must see."

FOR DISCUSSION AND REFLECTION

➤ Why do writers use loaded words in their writing? (Responses will vary but should include that they make arguments more effective and add zest to the style.)

➤ What do you notice about many of the loaded words found in this review? (Answers will vary. One answer is that many of them are absolutes and superlatives such as "great," "largest," "unsinkable," "intelligently," "flawlessly," "most," and "always.")

➤ What may slant an author's opinion one way or another? (Students may say education, background, age, gender, or relationship to the topic.)

W r i t i n g

QUICK ASSESS

Do students' responses:

✓ show that they recognize loaded words?

✓ understand how loaded words affect the reader?

✓ express an opinion about Ebert's review?

Most students will probably have seen the movie *Titanic* or will have already formed their own opinion of it. But once they analyze the loaded words in the review, Ebert's opinion should be obvious. Students are asked to write about the effects of Ebert's words.

READING AND WRITING EXTENSIONS

➤ Have students use loaded words as they write a review of their own for a movie that they like or dislike. Suggest that they read their reviews aloud in small groups, and ask their listeners to pick out the loaded language.

➤ Encourage students to collect travel brochures or advertisements and make lists of loaded words and phrases that give the information a positive bias.

See also Answer Key, page 123

Four The Emotional Appeal

Critical Reading

FOCUS

Anna Quindlen gets readers personally and emotionally involved with the homeless by telling a persuasive story:

"Her name was Ann, and we met in the Port Authority Bus Terminal several Januarys ago."

BACKGROUND

In "Homeless," Anna Quindlen wants to make the reader aware that "homeless" is not just an impersonal label but a word describing real people who, for whatever reason, are without homes. Quindlen is able to take a label and give it a face, make it a "somebody." She relates a personal anecdote that had a profound effect on her. Its stark, yet sensitive feeling floods the reader with a wash of emotion. As a result, the reader feels compelled to "do something" without even being asked.

➤ Quindlen uses a story as an "emotional hook" to snag the reader with its persuasive appeal. For instance, Quindlen says that her main character, Ann, didn't carry pictures of family or friends, or even a pet, but she did have a picture of a house: "She had a house, or at least once upon a time" had a home, a place with "those kinds of feelings that end up in cross-stitch and French knots on samplers over the years." Quindlen obtains the desired convincing result by sharing her poignant, emotional story and tapping into the core of every reader's heart.

FOR DISCUSSION AND REFLECTION

➤ How does Quindlen gain the reader's approval on this topic? (Answers may include that she conveys pity for people who don't have a home, empathy for those who have lost their "place," surprise that someone could live in a bus station, and so on.)

➤ What effect does Quindlen want to have on the reader of this essay? (Answers will vary but may include motivating readers to volunteer in a shelter, work at a food pantry, or contribute money or household goods to a charity.)

Writing

QUICK ASSESS

Do students' responses:

✔ recognize Quindlen's emotional appeal?

✔ evaluate its effectiveness?

Students are asked to respond to the story by recognizing the emotions that it evokes and illustrating them in a sketch. Brainstorm some ideas together with the class and remind them that artistic ability is not what's important. Making their sketches will help prepare them to evaluate the effectiveness of Quindlen's emotional appeals.

READING AND WRITING EXTENSIONS

➤ Ask the students to work with a partner to extend Quindlen's topic or one similar to it. Have them write a short story that appeals to the emotions, combining illustrations and text. Have students peer edit their stories in small groups or with younger children.

➤ Have students read Eve Bunting's *Fly Away Home*, a picture book about homelessness. Invite students to discuss its tone and theme.

Five The Tone

C r i t i c a l   R e a d i n g

FOCUS

Anna Quindlen's phrase is not a trite statement, but one of personal, heartfelt meaning:

"Home is where the heart is."

BACKGROUND

The conclusion of Anna Quindlen's "Homeless" is an excellent example of how emotion and tone can be used to advantage in persuasive writing. She uses very poignant images of children and old people and their sense of pride through ownership and place. One can't share her story without feeling compassion for those who have "No window to look out upon the world." Homelessness is an issue of human beings.

➤ Help students to see that without pleading or demanding, Quindlen makes her point subtly, yet firmly. Be sure that students understand that the purpose of persuasive writing is to convince the reader to see the writer's point of view and, perhaps, commit to action. The tone gives valuable clues about how the reader is supposed to feel.

FOR DISCUSSION AND REFLECTION

➤ What is Quindlen's tone? (Answers may vary, but students may describe it as sincere, serious, or from the heart.)

➤ How does the tone of Quindlen's essay compare to that of Mayor Morial's essay? (Students may say that it's more personal and heartfelt, less factual, more emotional.)

➤ What do you love about your home? (Answers will vary but encourage students to be very specific.)

➤ What images from Quindlen's essay will stay with you? (Responses will vary. Possible answers include children without a room, people sleeping on benches and in doorways, old people sitting on plastic chairs or lying on the sidewalk, and so on.)

W r i t i n g

QUICK ASSESS

Do students' responses:

✓ identify Quindlen's tone?

✓ explain how her tone affects their reading?

Once students start reacting to words and thinking about the feelings they evoke, they'll be ready to write about Quindlen's tone and explain how the tone affects them personally.

READING AND WRITING EXTENSIONS

➤ Invite students to select one of the photographs in their *Daybook* that intrigues them. Have them list words that describe the tone, the photographer's attitude toward his or her subject.

➤ Read to the class *Willy and the Soup Kitchen*, a children's book on the topic of the homeless and what people can do to help. Ask students to share their impressions with classmates.

See also Answer Key, page 123

Unit Overview

This unit invites students to immerse themselves in the world of science fiction and fantasy writer Ray Bradbury—his style, his craft, and his ideas. By reading excerpts from "Uncle Einar" and *The Martian Chronicles*, the short story "Fever Dream," and an introduction to a nonfiction piece, students begin to understand how Ray Bradbury mixes the real and the imaginary in his plots, characters, themes, and settings.

Literature Focus

	Lesson	Literature
1.	Bradbury's Characters	from "Uncle Einar" (Short Story)
2.	Bradbury's Settings	from *The Martian Chronicles* (Fiction)
3.	Bradbury's Plots	"Fever Dream" (Short Story)
4.	Bradbury's Themes	"Fever Dream" (Short Story)
5.	Bradbury's World	Introduction to *S Is for Space* (Nonfiction)

Reading Focus

1. Fantasy writers often create characters that are both realistic and fantastic at the same time.
2. When you read science fiction, notice how the author blends real and imaginary elements to create the setting.
3. Examining how writers of science fiction and fantasy move back and forth between the real and imaginary world can help you make predictions about story events.
4. Just like all fiction, science fiction and fantasy stories have themes. To find them, ask yourself, "What's it all about?"
5. Understanding the sources that inspire a writer can help you better understand his or her work.

Writing Focus

1. Write an original conversation between two characters in a short story.
2. Draw a setting based on the author's description.
3. Use details of the plot to predict what will happen next in "Fever Dream."
4. Identify and react to the theme of "Fever Dream."
5. Create a cover for Bradbury's biography that reflects the real and imaginary worlds in his works.

One Bradbury's Characters

Critical Reading

FOCUS

Ray Bradbury develops his characters by integrating real and imaginary qualities:

"His vast tarpaulin wings hummed nervously behind his indignant back."

BACKGROUND

Learning about Ray Bradbury's background sheds some light on his stories and the wonderful characters that fill them. Born in Waukegan, Illinois, in 1920, he was full of imagination as a young boy when he pounded out stories on his toy typewriter. He would write his own endings to stories, another example of his well-developed imagination. Comic books inspired him to write stories that skillfully mix fantasy and the real world. He even wrote historical fiction, such as *Drummer Boy of Shiloh*, which uses many accurate details to create a fine example of character in a Civil War setting.

➤ "Uncle Einar" is a good example of writing that melds the real and the make-believe into a strong, interesting character. The first clue in the selection that Uncle Einar isn't your everyday run-of-the-mill uncle is the description that his "vast tarpaulin wings hummed nervously behind his indignant back." Readers have to keep reading to figure out just what Bradbury is leading up to, but once they finish the piece, readers will have a marvelous image of Uncle Einar flying through the air, with the line of clothes trailing behind.

FOR DISCUSSION AND REFLECTION

➤ What is the relationship between Uncle Einar and his wife? (They have a good relationship; she knows how to cajole her husband into doing what she wants, and he puts up a minimum of fuss.)

➤ What are some of the real-world descriptions of Einar? (He's married, he has fingers, he jumps, he speaks, he weeps, and so on.)

➤ Why is Uncle Einar so appealing? (Bradbury makes him seem like a typical human and then throws in the green wings so matter-of-factly that the surprise is great fun.)

Writing

QUICK ASSESS

Do students' conversations:

✓ use a mixture of fantasy and real-world descriptions?

✓ keep Einar and his wife in character as they've been established in the selection?

Once students identify the real and imaginary characteristics of Uncle Einar, they'll use their notes to write his conversation with his wife upon tangling in the apple tree branches. Point out that Einar wasn't too keen on making the trip in the first place, so he'll more than likely blame his wife for the mishap.

READING AND WRITING EXTENSIONS

➤ Advise students that they have just been hired to paint a portrait of Uncle Einar and his wife. Have them base their painting on description in the selection, using a line from the piece for the caption. (Help inspire them by showing them Grant Wood's "American Gothic.")

➤ Ask students to gather information on insects or pictures of flying insects that might have been Bradbury's inspiration for this character.

See also Answer Key, page 123

Two Bradbury's Settings

Critical Reading

FOCUS

Ray Bradbury creates marvelous settings as he juggles the imaginary world with the real one:

"They had a house of crystal pillars on the planet Mars by the edge of an empty sea...."

BACKGROUND

Ray Bradbury explores human values and themes in a space-age society. He has won numerous awards and written more than 500 works, which include short stories, novels, plays, screenplays, television scripts, and verse. *The Martian Chronicles* was a television miniseries in 1980, and Mel Gibson is set to star in a remake of Bradbury's classic *Fahrenheit 451*, slated for release in 1999. The imaginary and real-world characteristics of his settings mesh so smoothly that the reader is totally drawn in to time and place that seem natural and believable. Students may find it ironic—and amusing—that Bradbury, such a master of futuristic science fiction, fears airplanes.

➤ In this lesson, students will have the opportunity to dissect one of Bradbury's settings. At several points, Bradbury describes it as ordinary, with a "house" and "walls" and "yard" and "blue sky." But intertwined with these familiarities are things like "the planet Mars," "crystal pillars," "magnetic dust," and "metal insects and electric spiders" that move us from realism to science fiction. All of a sudden the reader is transported to a "different" place that starts to take shape like an image that slowly develops on the Internet.

FOR DISCUSSION AND REFLECTION

➤ What clues suggest a "normal" setting? (Answers include a house with walls, a husband and wife, activities like cleaning house and painting pictures, desert sands, and blue sky.)

➤ Who or what is "Ylla"? (The main character of the excerpt is Mrs. K, whose first name is "Ylla" and whose husband's first name is Yll.)

➤ What might the "shining miracle" coming out of the sky be? (Answers could include a spaceship or a natural phenomenon.)

Writing

QUICK ASSESS

Do students' sketches:

✓ use details from the story?

✓ use appropriate color to support the mood?

✓ capture the mystery of Bradbury's world?

After students review their notes from reading "Ylla," advise them to try to sketch the entire scene with pencil first, as Bradbury has described it. Remind them that they need to include details from the story just as they would if they were writing a paragraph.

READING AND WRITING EXTENSIONS

➤ Suggest that the students write a continuation of the story, explaining why Mr. and Mrs. K were not happy and what Ylla saw in the sky. Have students share their stories in small groups.

➤ Read again the first paragraph of the selection and then invite students to imagine they are Mr. K's metal book of hieroglyphs. Have them write one of the tales that the book tells, paying special attention to describing the setting in vivid detail.

See also Answer Key, page 123

Three Bradbury's Plots

Critical Reading

FOCUS

Ray Bradbury combines real and imaginary details to structure the plots of his science fiction stories:

"The fingernails turned blue and then red. It took about an hour for it to change and when it was finished, it looked just like any ordinary hand. But it was not ordinary. It no longer was him any more."

BACKGROUND

As you begin "Bradbury's Plots," remind students that the plot of a story is the sequence of events that includes an introduction of characters and the conflict. Bradbury is such an expert at creating this sequencing that we move through these transitions without even realizing it. His plot plays out visually in our minds as if we were watching a movie screen. Bradbury brilliantly blends real and imaginary information so effortlessly that the reader is caught up in a web of total believability.

➤ Students should enjoy reading "Fever Dream" in Lesson Three so much that they won't want to stop in the middle. They will be eager to read on. Bradbury sucks us in with the "real" first paragraph, then starts to bring in subtle imaginary hints that the reader will attribute to "fever," such as when the "hand began to change" or "It did not change back. It was still something else." Point out to the students that Bradbury keeps including "real" information, such as the reference to amoebas and microbes, yet he lets readers make their own assumptions by not telling too much, so that their curiosity is heightened.

FOR DISCUSSION AND REFLECTION

➤ What is happening to Charles? (Answers may vary, but students should understand that Charles has a high fever and could possibly be hallucinating or he could be really "changing.")

➤ Is the story believable? (Some students will think it is because so many of the details are true facts. For instance, a high fever really does make your limbs feel hot and heavy. Ask students to describe how they felt when they had a high fever.)

➤ Do you think the doctor is implicated in the "change" somehow? (Answers may vary; he could be part of the problem, similar to the doctor in Steinbeck's *The Pearl*. Those pink pills might be poison.)

Writing

QUICK ASSESS

Do students' responses:

✓ list imaginary and real information?

✓ make a prediction about what will happen?

Students should make lots of notes to mark the spots where Bradbury moves back and forth between real and imaginary information in "Fever Dream." These notes will help them to understand Bradbury's technique for developing plot and also to make their predictions about what will happen next.

READING AND WRITING EXTENSIONS

➤ Invite students to write about similarities and differences between Stephen King's writings and Ray Bradbury's use of real and imaginary details in plot development.

➤ Suggest that students do some research on germs, cells, amoebas, and petrified wood to see if Bradbury has used them accurately in the story. Have them share their findings with the class.

Four Bradbury's Themes

Critical Reading

FOCUS

Ray Bradbury's themes skillfully weave together the real and the imaginary world:

"In the parlor, before the others entered, he quickly opened the bird cage, thrust his hand in, and petted the yellow canary, *once*. Then he shut the cage door, stood back, and waited."

BACKGROUND

Ray Bradbury's themes explore the human values of innocence (childhood) in contrast to those of experience (adulthood), the conflict between two worlds—real and imaginary—and the differences between the heart and the mind.

➤ In "Fever Dream," Bradbury investigates those differences and conflicts. The transformation that Charles experiences could be explained as an alien body takeover, a symbolic coming of age, or a combination of both. With adulthood comes responsibility, darkness, and pain. As an adult, Charles no longer wears the rose colored glasses of childhood. He has trouble letting go, shaking hands "for almost a minute," and says good-bye to a time that was "long ago."

FOR DISCUSSION AND REFLECTION

➤ Why do you think that the author set this story in the fall? (Answers may vary, but fall symbolizes the onset of winter, a dying or "resting" of life, and a time for change and metamorphosis.)

➤ Is Charles the same person at the end of the story as at the beginning? (Answers will vary, but some might say he is different after his fever experience, physically and mentally. Others may think that the whole experience was an hallucination or a bad dream perhaps to avoid school. Ask students to point to text evidence for their intepretations.)

➤ Why do you think that Charles reaches into the bird cage at the end of the story? (Answers will vary, but possibly his touch initiates change for the bird as well as himself.)

Writing

QUICK ASSESS

Do students' responses:

✓ show understanding of the real and imaginary scenes?

✓ explore the story's theme?

After students summarize the second part of "Fever Dream," they will summarize the story's theme and explain their own reactions to it. Remind students that there is no one "right" answer to the question, "What's this story all about?"

READING AND WRITING EXTENSIONS

➤ Invite students to read "Of Missing Persons" by Jack Finney and to compare the two authors' styles and themes.

➤ Have students brainstorm a list of other science fiction stories or movies in which real and imaginary worlds collide. Ask them to compare the themes of those works with that of "Fever Dream."

See also Answer Key, page 124

Five Bradbury's World

Critical Reading

FOCUS

Ray Bradbury writes with enthusiasm about life, respect for science, and a fascination with the future:

"My enthusiasm stood me well over the years. I have never tired of the rockets and the stars. I never cease enjoying the good fun of scaring heck out of myself with some of my weirder, darker, tales."

BACKGROUND

As they read Ray Bradbury's introduction to *S Is for Space*, students have an opportunity to consider the sources of inspiration for Bradbury's fantastic ideas, characters, and settings. His science fiction isn't just glamorous space adventure and special effects, but good science and good fiction. Bradbury's stories thrive on the fantastic and the marvelous, drawing upon authors such as Jules Verne (*20,000 Leagues Under the Sea*) and H.G. Wells (*War of the Worlds*) as inspiration. He obviously had a passion for life, a fascination with magic, a curiosity about space, and a love of reading—from Edgar Allan Poe to Robert Louis Stevenson.

➤ Students may have heard of Robert Heinlein and Isaac Asimov, two writers who dominated the science fiction field in the mid-twentieth century. Science fiction's popularity grew as developments in the production of nuclear energy and space exploration showed that much of the earlier science fiction writing was more realistic than people had once believed. With television shows and movies from *Star Trek* and *Star Wars* to *Men in Black* and *X-Files*, the appeal of science fiction continues to be enormous.

FOR DISCUSSION AND REFLECTION

➤ Why would Flash Gordon and Buck Rogers influence Bradbury? (They were early science fiction characters who traveled in space.)

➤ What influence would Jules Verne and H.G. Wells bring to Bradbury's work? (They were both early science fiction and adventure writers.)

➤ What does Bradbury mean when he says that "You who read, and I who write, are very much the same"? (Responses will vary but should focus on the powers of imagination.)

Writing

QUICK ASSESS

Do students' book covers:

✔ include a sketch and a brief description?

✔ show an understanding of Bradbury's real and imaginary worlds?

Once students think about the sources Bradbury mentions in his introduction, they should have some excellent ideas from which to create their book cover. Suggest that they make some preliminary sketches and look at sample "blurbs" from other book jackets before making their designs.

READING AND WRITING EXTENSIONS

➤ Invite students to imagine that fifty years from now, when they have become famous writers, they will have to explain what books they read in their childhood that had a great influence on them. Have them jot down several titles, explaining briefly what impressed them about the work.

➤ Ask students to write their own short stories of life on Mars, using original settings based on current scientific facts, characters, and plot.

ANSWER KEY

A n s w e r   K e y

Most activities in the *Daybook* ask for open-ended, creative responses. As a result, only selected activities for which specific answers are possible are included here. The intent is to help you, the teacher, by clarifying a possible or partial response to the question, not to specify the one complete, true answer. Answers are given here only for teachers who want further clarification of specific activities.

PAGE 18: Students' charts will differ. The following is one example:

Victor	Teresa	Mr. Bueller
He tried to impress Teresa by saying he already knows French.	She was impressed that Victor could speak French.	He was happy that his student spoke French, but quickly realized that Victor had lied.
He was embarrassed that he couldn't really speak French. He was afraid to face Teresa after class and that Mr. Bueller would say something about the lie.	She didn't notice that Victor couldn't really speak French.	He was happy that he had a student with whom to speak French, but he quickly realized that Victor had lied.

PAGE 19: Students' paragraphs about elements of Soto's perspective will vary. Following is a general example:

In "Seventh Grade," Gary Soto focuses on Victor's emotions. He writes of Victor's like for Teresa and shows how important it is to Victor that he is liked by Teresa and others. Victor blushes when he talks to Teresa and is happy that when he scowls, a girl watches him. He tries to impress Teresa in French class by lying about speaking French. Soto also shows how embarrassed Victor is when he can't answer Mr. Bueller's questions in French, but how happy Victor is that Teresa hasn't noticed.

PAGE 22: Students' charts will vary. Following is a sample chart:

Elements of Craft	"Oranges"	"Seventh Grade"
strong images	"Frost cracking/Beneath my steps";"face bright/With rouge";"candies/Tiered like bleachers"	Michael's scowl; Victor's eyes meeting Teresa's; Victor's embarrassment in French class
vivid descriptions of feelings	feelings left for the reader to interpret	Victor's feelings for Teresa and his embarrassment in French class
humorous phrases or expressions	It's not a humorous poem.	Victor and Michael scowling to impress girls;"Frenchie oh wewe gee in September"
realistic characterization	The speaker acts like any boy who is proud of his girlfriend.	Characters display feelings and interests of most seventh-grade students.

PAGE 25: Students' answers will vary but should include:

Soto came from a family that didn't have a lot of money for extras. He made himself do the work even though he didn't want to because he wanted his mother to think well of him, and he did need the money. He had a rich imagination, which he used to escape boredom.

PAGE 26: Students' charts will vary but might look like this:

"Seventh Grade"	"Oranges"
Victor and Michael pick grapes to earn their fall clothes. Victor daydreams about Teresa, a "would-be girlfriend."	The speaker doesn't have much money for extras.

PAGE 29: Students' predictions will vary. A sample prediction follows:

No one bothers Latoya on Freshman Day.

PAGE 34: 1. Topic: California is installing new, safer equipment on its playgrounds.

2. The authors explore whether it is good that the equipment is being replaced, interviewing people who used the old ones and are using the new ones.

The authors of this article state that although some people prefer the old playgrounds, the new equipment is safer and will eliminate serious injuries, though not all minor ones.

PAGE 42: Students' tables and their descriptions of the mood change will differ. Following is one example:

morning	afternoon
Sunlight piercing the foliage	Shade
Butterflies	Stillness; "solemnity that brooded"
Sleeping village	Sense of loneliness

PAGE 44: Students' responses will differ. A sample answer follows:

Huck is a dynamic character because he does not follow society's rules, but instead does as he pleases. He doesn't do the same thing or dress the same or act in the same way every day.

Tom	Huckleberry
Respectable, respectful, naïve, polite, conventional, envious	Loner, castoff, juvenile deliquent, wild, undisciplined

Tom and Huck have come from very different backgrounds: Tom has grown up with nicer clothes and more parental discipline than Huck. Huck comes and goes as he pleases and dresses in ragtag clothes.

Tom and Huck are alike, though, in that they are both boys with the same interests, such as their fascination with the dead cat.

PAGE 47: Students will choose different parts of the story to rewrite. Stories might include the following points:

• Mrs. Kim worrying about Hideyo's feet

• Mr. Kim wondering what would happen to his family if they were caught sheltering Hideyo, then coming to a resolute decision about protecting him

• Hee Wang wondering what would have happened if he were the one separated from his family as Hideyo is

PAGE 50:

Rising Action: from the point when the American notices the hostess's actions and the servant with the bowl of milk to the point when he challenges the guests to remain still

Climax: the point at which everyone sits still and waits

Falling Action: the point where the cobra emerges and moves toward the bowl of milk, while the guests who see the cobra begin to scream to the point when the American questions the hostess

PAGE 51:

Students' charts will vary. Following is an example:

Character	Lesson
the Colonel	One can't generalize about the behavior of all men or all women in a crisis.
the girl	Mrs. Wynnes proved her theory that women could be calm in a crisis.
the American	He learned that he could be calm in the face of a crisis; he learned that Mrs. Wynnes had incredible self-control.
Mrs. Wynnes	She learned that she could control an urge to react wildly in a crisis.

PAGE 56:

Students' paragraphs will differ, but they should contain the information that Robert Peterson admires Jackie Robinson both for what he accomplished in the world of baseball (a career that led to induction into the Hall of Fame) and what he accomplished for African Americans (first African American to become a major-league ball player).

PAGE 57:

Students' charts will vary, but the beginning of their additions might look like this:

Incident	What the Incident Reveals About Robinson
Robinson recieves hate mail.	Robinson took a courageous stand.
People screamed racial slurs at him.	Robinson wanted to hit these people but held back. He was able to focus on playing the game, and playing it well.

PAGE 59:

Students' descriptions of Robinson's attitude should include the following points:

• He thought intolerance was childish.

• He did not ask for special treatment or support. He expected to prove himself in spring training, and he asked only that other players, like Reese, give him a fair chance to play.

• He wanted friendship and acceptance from his fellow players, just as anyone would want, and he appreciated finding both of these in his relationship with Pee Wee Reese.

PAGE 61:

The Venn diagrams will differ based on the points in students' own news articles. Some of the advantages of biographical writing they might list would be that it allows the reader to really know the writer's thoughts and feelings and gives the reader an insider's knowledge of historical events. Some disadvantages are that autobiographical writing gives the reader only one side of the story of any event, and it will not include details that are unknown to the writer.

PAGE 64: Students' paragraphs should include the information that Sharon Robinson's account reveals the personal side of Jackie Robinson—his home life, his role as a parent—which is not revealed in the excerpts in Lessons One and Two.

Students' charts will differ. Following is one example:

Characteristic	Source(s)
Determination	B, A
Talent as a ball player	B
Wish to fit in, to find acceptance for himself	B, A
Search for tolerance for all African Americans	B, A, PA
Patience	PA

PAGE 65: Clifton compares Robinson to a baseball being hit around a ballpark. She suggests that Robinson was strong, determined, and brave, a trailblazer, and a symbol of the larger struggle for racial equality.

PAGE 67: Students' charts will vary. Here is a sample chart:

Genre	Strengths	Limitations
biography	gives the story of events from all sides	often has a bias, either in favor of or against the subject, so the writing is not objective
autobiography	written by the subject, so the reader finds out what the person actually saw or felt during any event	Reader gaining only the subject's perspective
personal account	gives more information, an insider's view, about the subject from someone who actually knew him or her	has a personal bias that comes through in the writing
poem	can portray the subject as larger than life, heroically, very picturesquely	abstract and easily misunderstood, not straightforward

PAGE 71: A sample list of images from the poem might include:

sight: summer, church picnic, mountains

sound: gospel music

taste: corn, okra, greens, cabbage, barbecue, buttermilk, ice-cream

smell: barbecue, buttermilk

touch: barefooted, warm, bed

PAGE 82: Students' answers will vary. One example might be the following:

Katie's mother knows she is dying and that Katie will probably take her death badly. Katie is young, and her mother wants her not to grieve endlessly but to go on to live a full life. The empty box symbolizes the young Katie, who still has her life's future experiences, with which she can "fill herself up."

PAGE 84: Carlson's thesis statement: "Practicing random kindness is an effective way to get in touch with the joy of giving without expecting anything in return.

PAGE 93: Students' charts will differ. Following is an example:

What the opposition says	Sojourner Truth's response
Women need to be taken care of.	"Nobody ever helps me into carriages, or over mud-puddles, or gives me any best place! And ain't I a woman?"
Women are weak.	"I have plowed and planted, and gathered into barns, and no man could head me! And ain't I a woman? I could work as much and eat as much as a man—when I could get it—and bear the lash as well! And ain't I a woman?"
Women don't bear pain well.	"I have borne thirteen children, and seen them most all sold off to slavery, and when I cried out with my mother's grief, none but Jesus heard! And ain't I a woman?"
Women aren't as smart as men.	"What's that got to do with women's rights or Negro's rights?"
Only men are Christlike; Christ wasn't a woman.	"Where did your Christ come from? Where did your Christ come from? From god and a woman! Man had nothing to do with him."

PAGE 95: Students' charts will vary. Here are some samples of how these writers address and persuade their audiences:

L'Amour	Carlson	Truth
Uses "we," as in "we're all in this together" Addresses "nay-sayers" so as to explain and dismiss their arguments Presents his thesis as inevitable	Addresses audience as "you" to make the writing more personal and direct Gives many different examples of random acts of kindness to answer any reader's objection of "I can't think of anything to do" Gives the impression of expecting a disinterested audience	Like L'Amour, addresses the opposing arguments and dismisses them with an explanation of her point of view Addresses the arguments of individual men in her audience ("That man over there," "that little man in black there"), so it's obvious she's confronting the actual authors of those arguments in a possibly hostile audience

PAGE 100: Students' writings will differ, but some might include that Uchida thinks Japan is a country of hard-working people who have faith that they will be rewarded for hard work with prosperity.

PAGE 101:   Students will answer this question differently. Some might say that although "The Princess of Light" may not yet know who she is, she knows that she has a home with and belongs to the old man and old woman, who will love her and take care of her whether she brings them riches or not.

PAGE 103:   Students might list any of the following about Uchida:

- Born in California and is Japanese American
- Loved and respected her parents
- Felt like an outsider (or a "foreigner") most of the time she was growing up
- Experienced ignorance and intolerance from other Americans

PAGE 104:   Student's charts will differ. Some sample points appear in the chart below:

I am Japanese	I am Japanese American	I am American
My name is Japanese. My face is Japanese. My Japanese parents taught me their values and shared with me their spirit and soul.	I look Japanese, but I speak English. I want to be friends with my neighbors.	I was born in California and grew up in America. I love my country as much as any American. I recite the Pledge of Allegiance.

PAGE 107:   Students' webs will vary. Here is a sample:

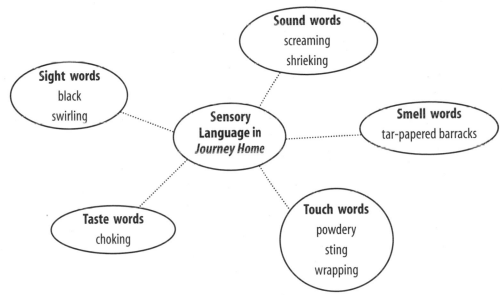

PAGE 111:   Students' summaries will vary but should include these ideas:
Uchida writes to give a voice to Japanese Americans and to familiarize non-Asians with their lives and values.

PAGE 112: Students will write about various aspects of Uchida's work. A sample organizer might look like this:

What she writes about	In what book?	What lesson does she want to teach?
Her experiences as a young Japanese American girl in America	*The Invisible Thread*	That although her face and name are Japanese, she was just as American as any other person born in the U.S.A.
Life in an internment camp during WWII	*Journey Home*	That Japanese Americans were made to live in conditions that were oppressive and inhuman
Second-generation Japanese Americans leaving internment camps for new lives outside the camps	*Desert Exile*	That older Japanese Americans sacrificed much so that their young people might have better lives

PAGE 116: *Who are the people involved?*

A six-year-old girl, her mother, and a group of ornithologists

Where and when do the events take place?

The mother's house, one summer in the 1950s

What happened and how did it happen?

(Students' answers will vary, but they should include that the ornithologists used the little girl's feverish body to hatch a group of wild turkey eggs.)

The actual writing of the news leads will vary, but students should include the above points.

PAGE 124: Students' charts will differ. Here's a sample chart:

Laurie's mother is obsessed with Charles.	Laurie's father is slow to become interested in Charles.	Laurie is amused by Charles's behavior, and he brags about it.
She can't stop asking questions about him. She allows "Charles" to become an institution. She can't wait to meet his mother.	He doesn't ask many questions about Charles. He doesn't show much interest until he hears that Charles swore in school.	He reports all details to his parents. He shouts out these details almost gleefully.

PAGE 132: Students' descriptions and details will vary. Following is a sample:

DETAIL: "Wildflowers bloomed in meadows"

DETAIL: "forests of firs stretched up the slopes"

DETAIL: They predicted it would erupt again before the year 2000.

Main Idea:
Most people saw the mountain as a green and pleasant place,

but geologists saw it as a dangerous volcano about to erupt.

DETAIL: elk and deer lived there

DETAIL: It had erupted in the past.

DETAIL: a young volcano "one of the most active in the Cascade Range"

PAGE 135: Students' generalizations and supporting details will differ. Here are examples:

By gathering different types of information, about volcanoes, some scientists may be able to predict when a volcanic eruption will probably occur.

Geologists looked at past eruptions of Mount St. Helens.

Geologists took samples of ash and gases from the mountain to find clues about what was happening inside.

Geologists measured the mountains' bulge to watch for rapid growth, meaning a possible eruption.

PAGE 139: Students will list different causes and effects in their charts. Here's a sample chart:

Effects		Causes
Mr. Misenheimer started his garden.	because	He wanted to make a little bit of the world a bit nicer.
Haeja worked with Mr. Misenheimer.	because	She had always dreamed of living near lots of flowers.
Haeja and the Misenheimers became good friends.	because	Haeja and the Misenheimers had no other family.
Haeja still works in the garden.	because	Haeja honors the memory of Mr. Misenheimer.
When Haeja first stopped, she stayed in the garden for the afternoon.	because	Mr. Misenheimer came to greet her and talked to her.

PAGE 140: Students' general and follow-up statements will differ. Following are examples:

1. *Specific:* A person might "plant love and kindness" by visiting a sick child in the hospital.

2. *Conclusion:* One result that might "grow" from those actions could be that I make a new friend.

PAGE 141: 1. *Specific:* I could pay "loving attention" to a garden by watering and weeding it.

2. *Conclusion:* If I do that, the earth will reward me by helping the flowers in the garden grow tall and strong.

PAGE 144:   Students will design different Venn diagrams and come to differing conclusions, but here is what one student might determine:

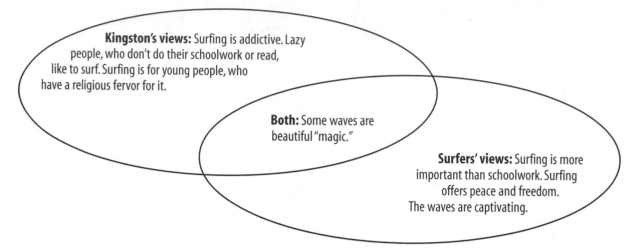

Kingston's views: Surfing is addictive. Lazy people, who don't do their schoolwork or read, like to surf. Surfing is for young people, who have a religious fervor for it.

Both: Some waves are beautiful "magic."

Surfers' views: Surfing is more important than schoolwork. Surfing offers peace and freedom. The waves are captivating.

Conclusion: Both Kingston and the surfers believe that the ocean is an exciting place, but Kingston thinks the boys go too far in their devotion to surfing.

PAGE 148:   Students might list the following conflicts:

• Esther liked living alone, and now she has Michael in her house; Michael feels like a lonely outsider.

• Esther is very outgoing, and Michael wants to keep to himself.

• Esther is an adult, and Michael is a 14-year-old boy; they don't have much in common.

• Michael is grieving, and Esther is impatient with his grieving process.

PAGE 149:   Students' tables might look like this:

Michael	Aunt Esther
He thinks she is selfish.	He speaks disrespectfully.
She's a complainer.	He is sullen and broods.
She's prejudiced.	He hates her and living with her.
He sometimes hates her but doesn't want to.	
He doesn't feel he belongs with her.	

Students will sympathize with different characters for different reasons. Following is a sample prediction of what will happen next in the story:

They might try to talk more about their feelings, or they might find something to do together that they both like and can talk about.

PAGE 152: Students will have differing ideas about Michael's inner conflicts and what he resolves by the end of the story. Following are some samples:

wants to be left alone vs. feels lonely

wants not to hate Aunt Esther vs. hates her

wants her to leave him alone vs. wants her to be interested in him and his pet

By the end of the story, Michael doesn't hate Esther, and he wants to be friendlier toward her. They are both interested in Sluggo.

PAGE 157: Students will have different impressions of the narrator. Following might be one student's opinion:

She doesn't feel that it is special to be Indian. She has no use for tradition. She hates rituals. She doesn't want to do things just because they are expected of her. She wants to make her own place in the world.

PAGE 160: Students will cite different parts of the story in defining Father's character. Here are examples:

compassion
takes the baby from the woman and helps her hold the baby correctly

sense of humor
laughs at having his boots on the wrong feet

perseverance
unsure of what to do but sets out to help others anyway

Students will also have differing ideas about Miss Whitlaw. One student might say the following:

She wants to help in time of crisis, but social conventions, such as being properly clothed before she helps, are still important to her.

PAGE 164: Students' comparison charts might look like this:

Style Choice	Jack London	Scott O'Dell
Point of view	3rd person—told by someone outside the story	1st person—told by the person in the story
Length of sentences	long, with several clauses	short
Type of language (informal or formal? simple or complex?)	formal and complex	simple and informal, as a person would speak
Are there figurative expressions, such as similes and metaphors?	no	yes (water made noises that "seemed angry" or like "people laughing")
Tone—how the writing "sounds" (suspenseful, scary, exciting, and so on)	suspenseful, exciting	peaceful, quiet

PAGE 167: Students' word choices to describe Wing Tek Lum's poem and attitude will vary. Following is an example:

The poem's tone is quietly happy.

The words are informal.

The impression that this poem gives is: Wing Tek Lum likes America for its diversity.

Lum's feeling about America is: It's a good place to live. Everyone can live here but can still be different from one another.

PAGE 171: Students should have placed an X next to the stage direction above the Driver's second speech on page 168.

They should have placed a Y on page 170, next to the Traveler's line, "Oh, I see."

Students' Venn diagrams will differ but should include many of the main ideas expressed here:

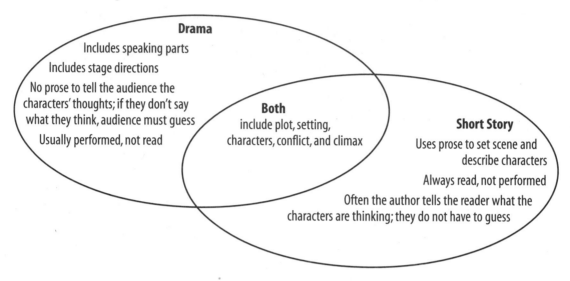

Drama
Includes speaking parts
Includes stage directions
No prose to tell the audience the characters' thoughts; if they don't say what they think, audience must guess
Usually performed, not read

Both
include plot, setting, characters, conflict, and climax

Short Story
Uses prose to set scene and describe characters
Always read, not performed
Often the author tells the reader what the characters are thinking; they do not have to guess

PAGE 172: Students' opinions will vary, but they should include that the title, "Direction," has two meanings: sending someone in a geographic direction or giving someone advice. The lines of the poem alternate between the two meanings.

PAGE 177: Students' answers will vary, but they might include the following:

• The speaker thought of his father as a "giant," a great man. A real giant would need many people to carry his coffin because of his size; a great man would deserve many pallbearers as a sign of respect.

• The speaker might mean that his father was so popular that one hundred men wanted to carry his coffin as a sign of their grief and love for him.

Following is a sample chart comparing the speaker's childhood and adult views:

Objects/People	Childhood View	Adult View
hills	"great mountains"	"mere hills"
rivers	"raging rivers"	"gentle streams"
road	wide, leading to exciting places	crooked and dusty, leading to the cemetery
father	a giant of a man	view unchanged

PAGE 180: Poe filled "Annabel Lee" with sound devices, and students' response notes will differ. Some examples might include:

• He again repeats "loved" and "love" in the second stanza, re-emphasizing his feelings.

• "Chilling and killing" in stanza four is an ominous rhyme and makes her sound as if she died a very quick death.

• He changes the rhyme and rhythm in the last stanza. The last two lines rhyme, giving the end of a poem a mournful sound.

PAGE 187: Students will choose different qualities to include in their webs. Following are some choices:

• legs, feet, mouth, and skin

• ability to study

• ability to hear

• ability to see

• ability to write a diary

• ability to remember

PAGE 192: Throughout the piece, Morial says that the curfew is a major tool in helping New Orleans fight crime by teenagers. Students' writings should include this point.

PAGE 197: Students' lists of Ebert's loaded words might include the following: majestically, flawlessly, intelligently, strongly, spellbinding, convincing, seamless, balanced. Students will finish the sentence that follows in different ways, depending on their impressions from the review.

PAGE 202: Students will write of different emotions, depending on how Quindlen's writing affected them. They will also differ on their opinions of her tone, but some words they may use are angry, sad, disbelieving (that people would have to live in this way), indignant, or discouraged.

PAGE 205: Students will ascribe different characteristics to Uncle Einar, both real and imaginary, but some might include the following:

Imaginary	Real-World
has green tarpaulin wings	has hands and fingers
cries acid tears	wears clothes
	gets angry

PAGE 207: Students' descriptions of Ylla will differ but should include some of the following aspects: a crystal house with pillars; a desolate, sandy landscape with some trees and an empty sea; hot winds; blue sky.

PAGE 211:   Students' plot lines should look something like this:

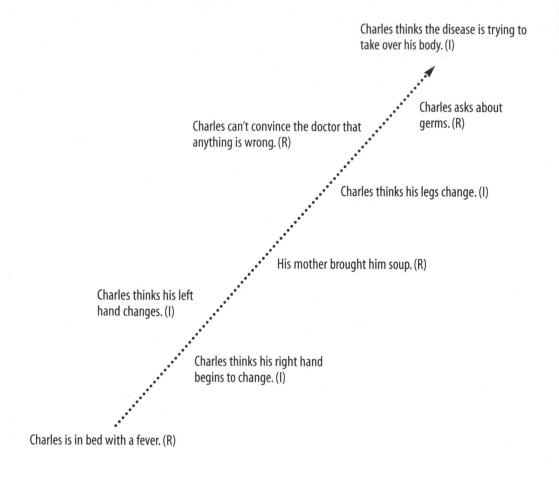

Charles thinks the disease is trying to take over his body. (I)

Charles asks about germs. (R)

Charles can't convince the doctor that anything is wrong. (R)

Charles thinks his legs change. (I)

His mother brought him soup. (R)

Charles thinks his left hand changes. (I)

Charles thinks his right hand begins to change. (I)

Charles is in bed with a fever. (R)

Students' predictions of what will happen next in the story will differ.

PAGE 215:   Students' interpretations of what actually happened in the second half of "Fever Dream" will differ. Following is an example of a student summary:

Charles became more and more certain that something was taking over his body. He could not convince the doctor or his parents that it was happening. Meanwhile, he continues to sicken until the fever affects every part of his body. Then one day he suddenly becomes well. The doctor and his parents are amazed at his recovery. He seems to act differently, but no one really notices because they are so glad that he is well.

Students will also differ on the theme of the story. One theme statement might be:

People are not always who they seem to be.

I n d e x

Teacher's Guide page numbers are in parentheses following pupil's edition page numbers.

Lesson Title Index

Literature Index